Fo e

Not t room

DATE DUE		
OCT 0 2 1997		
OCT 0 2 1997		
OCT 0 9 1997		

WITHDRAWN

THE NEW FLORIDA ATLAS

PATTERNS OF THE SUNSHINE STATE

Dr. Roland Wood
Department of Geography
Florida State University

Dr. Edward A. Fernald
Department of Geography
Florida State University

Preface

Florida and its resources have long been subjects of major concern for the Geography Department at the Florida State University. The Department has been a center for teaching about Florida, while the major functions of the Florida Resources and Environmental Analysis Center have been resource research and service to agencies of the state. It was out of this teaching and research activity that the authors identified the pressing need for a new Florida atlas to up-date the fine work put out in 1964 as the *Atlas of Florida.*

The New Florida Atlas: Patterns of the Sunshine State was undertaken in 1972 to provide a current reference atlas of Florida utilizing the data compiled for the United States Census of Agriculture, 1969, and the United States Census of Population, 1970. These sources, in addition to the most current data provided by the various agencies of the State of Florida, help make *The New Florida Atlas* an up-to-date reference source.

The composition of the Atlas provides a rational outline of Florida's cultural and physical resources. It is a shared belief of the authors that its citizens are Florida's most important resource. Following this rationale the first major section deals with the characteristics of Florida's population. Geographers have long understood that the physical characteristics of a place suggest and limit man's activities. These topics make up a major section.

A major strength of *The New Florida Atlas,* and the section that has the largest number of original maps, is the water section. It is important that Floridians begin to understand the importance of this life-giving mineral.

A major section dealing with various aspects of man's economic activity including transportation, tourism, land use, types of economic activity, and employment in the state is followed by a brief section on the spatial distribution of Indian tribes, political boundaries and historical maps of population density.

A final section deals with the availability and scales of topographic maps and aerial photography of the State of Florida.

Utilization of the Atlas is envisioned by governmental officials of all levels, businessmen whose success is dependent upon a knowledge of the state and students and teachers who depend upon sound data for an analysis of Florida, its problems and its prospects.

Teachers are encouraged to use *The New Florida Atlas* not only as a source of information about the state, but as a tool for the development of patterns and trends, and as a stepping stone to creative thinking about Florida and it's resources. In short, *The New Florida Atlas: Patterns of theSunshine State* will hopefully be used by Florida citizens to make intelligent decisions regarding the preservation, use and development of Florida's cultural and physical resources.

Acknowledgements

Publication of an atlas of this scope requires people with varied abilities and talents. Foremost are four geography students of Florida State University. Jay Baker was in charge of data acquisition during the early stages of compilation. Geoffrey W. Kaiser and Jonathan Curry worked on all phases of compilation and design during most of the one and one half years required to complete this atlas, and Jeffrey Loeding assisted in compilation.

Dr. Neal G. Lineback of the Department of Geology and Geography, University of Alabama, and Mr. C. Tim Traylor of the Department of Geography, University of Southern Mississippi, gave the authors most useful advice during the planning phase. Dr. William F. Tanner of the Department of Geology, Florida State University, gave valuable advice on maps in the water section, the maps of geology, soils and landforms, and contributed the coastal energy map. James T. Bradley, Climatologist for the State of Florida, gave a great deal of assistance with the climate section. Dr. Hale Smith of the Florida State University Department of Anthropology assisted the authors with the maps of Indian tribes and Dr. J. Leitch Wright, Department of History, Florida State University, assisted in compilation of maps in the history section. Dr. John H. Davis, Professor Emeritus, University of Florida, helped compile and edit the map of natural vegetation. William H. Kuyper of the Florida Department of Transportation provided information on aerial photography coverage. Marianne Donnell, Map Librarian, Florida State University, was most helpful in providing source maps. Numerous other individuals, especially employees of various agencies of the State of Florida, provided data. Without such cooperation, it would have been impossible to produce this atlas.

Finally, we wish to thank members of the staff of Trend House for their contributions to this work.

R.W.
E.A.F.

Contents

Physical Characteristics

Water

Climate

Transportation and Communication

Tourism and Recreation

Economic Activity

Agriculture

Forestry

Commercial Fishing

Manufacturing

Employment

Health

History

Topographic Mapping

Aerial Photography

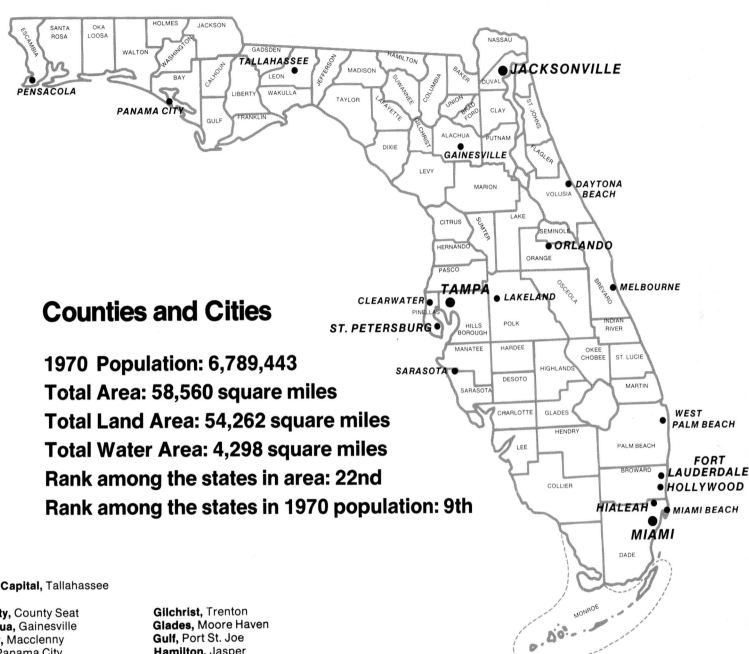

Counties and Cities

1970 Population: 6,789,443

Total Area: 58,560 square miles

Total Land Area: 54,262 square miles

Total Water Area: 4,298 square miles

Rank among the states in area: 22nd

Rank among the states in 1970 population: 9th

State Capital, Tallahassee

County, County Seat
Alachua, Gainesville
Baker, Macclenny
Bay, Panama City
Bradford, Starke
Brevard, Titusville
Broward, Fort Lauderdale
Calhoun, Blountstown
Charlotte, Punta Gorda
Citrus, Inverness
Clay, Green Cove Springs
Collier, Naples
Columbia, Lake City
Dade, Miami
DeSoto, Arcadia
Dixie, Cross City
Duval, Jacksonville
Escambia, Pensacola
Flagler, Bunnell
Franklin, Apalachicola
Gadsden, Quincy

Gilchrist, Trenton
Glades, Moore Haven
Gulf, Port St. Joe
Hamilton, Jasper
Hardee, Wauchula
Hendry, LaBelle
Hernando, Brooksville
Highlands, Sebring
Hillsborough, Tampa
Holmes, Bonifay
Indian River, Vero Beach
Jackson, Marianna
Jefferson, Monticello
Lafayette, Mayo
Lake, Tavares
Lee, Fort Myers
Leon, Tallahassee
Levy, Bronson
Liberty, Bristol
Madison, Madison
Manatee, Bradenton

Marion, Ocala
Martin, Stuart
Monroe, Key West
Nassau, Fernandina
Okaloosa, Crestview
Okeechobee, Okeechobee
Orange, Orlando
Osceola, Kissimmee
Palm Beach, West Palm Beach
Pasco, Dade City
Pinellas, Clearwater
Polk, Bartow
Putnam, Palatka

St. Johns, St. Augustine
St. Lucie, Fort Pierce
Santa Rosa, Milton
Sarasota, Sarasota
Seminole, Sanford
Sumter, Bushnell
Suwannee, Live Oak
Taylor, Perry
Union, Lake Butler
Volusia, Deland
Wakulla, Crawfordville
Walton, Defuniak Springs
Washington, Chipley

Population

Population growth patterns indicate a 1980 total population of approximately 9.4 million for the State of Florida. Phenomenal population growth of 78 percent between 1950 and 1960 decreased to 37 percent between 1960 and 1970. In 1973 projections show the State will maintain this 37 percent growth through 1980. Florida continues to be the fastest growing of the 10 most populous states in the nation with a population increase of over 4 percent per year.

Florida gained 26,610 residents in 1972 by natural increase, or births over deaths. In mid 1973 the birth rate in Florida was 14.1 per 1,000 population. The death rate in the 1970's rose slightly to 10.9 per 1,000 in 1973. In each case, both race groups contributed to the change. In addition to the natural increase total, it is estimated that Florida is gaining approximately 5,000 new residents weekly through immigration from other states and foreign countries.

In spite of the continued high rate of population growth, 6 North Florida counties lost population between 1960 and 1970. The age structure of Florida's population differs from that of the United States in that 25.8 percent of its population is under 15 years old which is below the national average while 14.6 percent of the population is over 65. This is much higher than the national average.

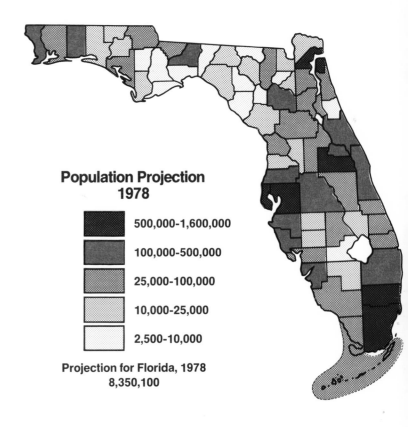

**Population Projection
1978**

■	500,000-1,600,000
■	100,000-500,000
▨	25,000-100,000
▫	10,000-25,000
□	2,500-10,000

**Projection for Florida, 1978
8,350,100**

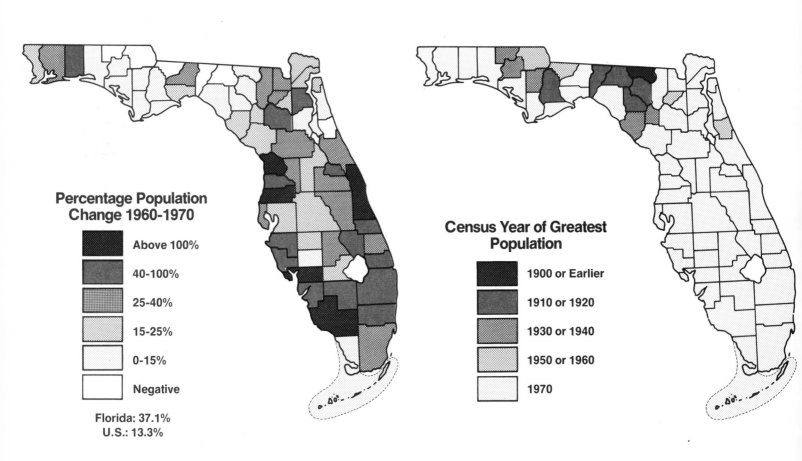

**Percentage Population
Change 1960-1970**

■	Above 100%
■	40-100%
▨	25-40%
▫	15-25%
□	0-15%
□	Negative

**Florida: 37.1%
U.S.: 13.3%**

**Census Year of Greatest
Population**

■	1900 or Earlier
■	1910 or 1920
▨	1930 or 1940
▫	1950 or 1960
□	1970

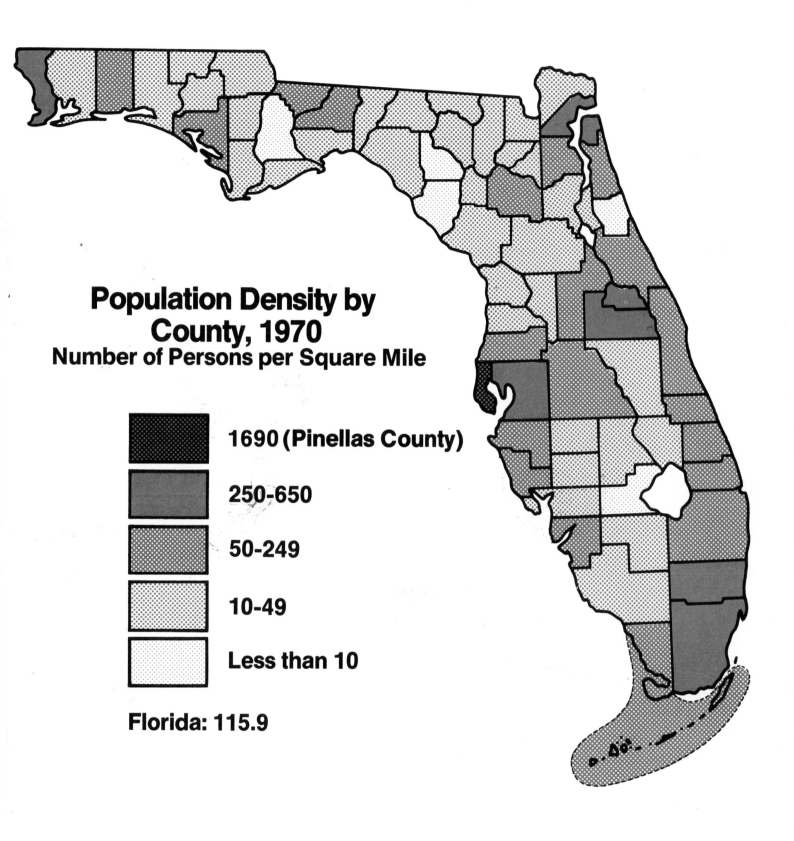

Population Density by County, 1970
Number of Persons per Square Mile

1690 (Pinellas County)

250-650

50-249

10-49

Less than 10

Florida: 115.9

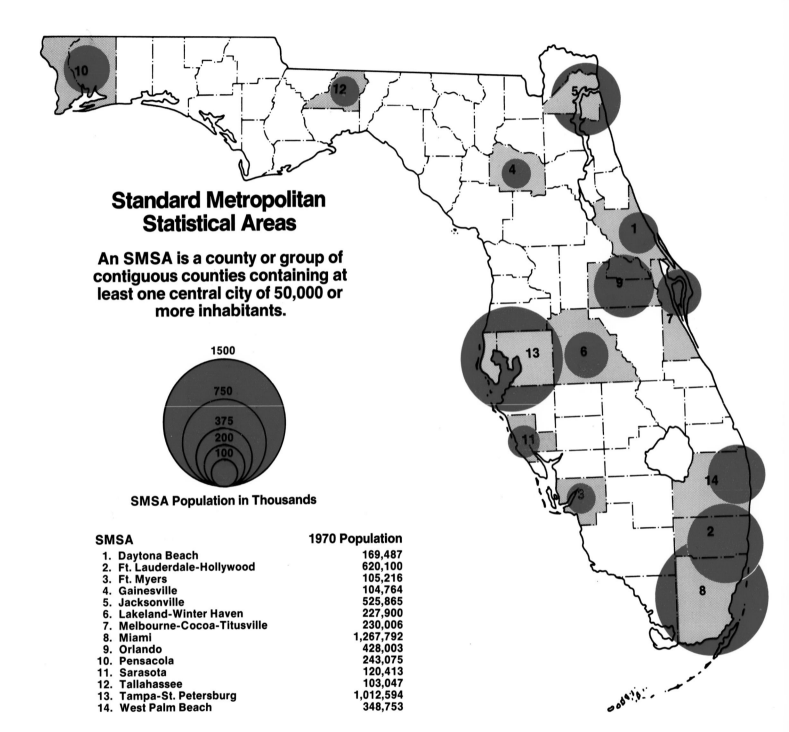

Standard Metropolitan Statistical Areas

An SMSA is a county or group of contiguous counties containing at least one central city of 50,000 or more inhabitants.

1500
750
375
200
100

SMSA Population in Thousands

SMSA	1970 Population
1. Daytona Beach	169,487
2. Ft. Lauderdale-Hollywood	620,100
3. Ft. Myers	105,216
4. Gainesville	104,764
5. Jacksonville	525,865
6. Lakeland-Winter Haven	227,900
7. Melbourne-Cocoa-Titusville	230,006
8. Miami	1,267,792
9. Orlando	428,003
10. Pensacola	243,075
11. Sarasota	120,413
12. Tallahassee	103,047
13. Tampa-St. Petersburg	1,012,594
14. West Palm Beach	348,753

Population Increase: Standard Metropolitan Statistical Areas

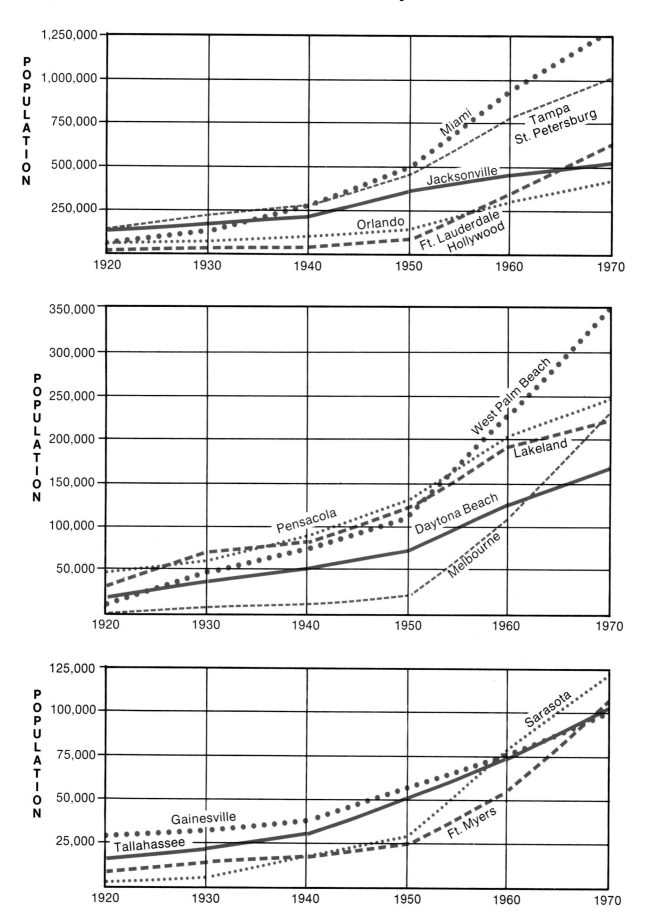

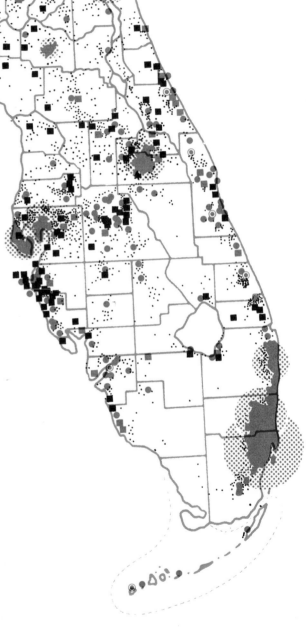

Population Distribution

Urbanized Areas

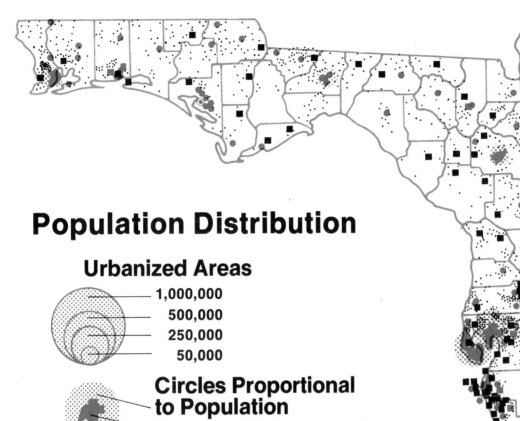

— 1,000,000
— 500,000
— 250,000
— 50,000

Circles Proportional to Population
Extent of Urbanized Areas

⊙ 25,000-50,000
■ 10,000-25,000
● 2,500-10,000

Rural Population

■ 1,000-2,500
• 500 inhabitants

VITAL STATISTICS. Final figures for 1970 are used for the vital statistics maps. The following discussions include comparative analyses for preliminary figures for 1971 which had not been summarized in final form.

The 1971 provisional figures showed an increase in total births of 1.8 percent over 1970 figures (116,453 versus 114,400). However, after showing a rise for the years 1969 and 1970, the rate per 1,000 population remained almost unchanged (16.7 versus 16.6). This is the result of the drop in the white birth rate (from 15.0 in 1970 to 14.7 in 1971) while the rate for nonwhites continued to rise (up from 26.1 to 26.9).

Based on provisional data, 75,860 Florida residents died during 1971. This was the all-time high for the 25th consecutive year, although the death rate of 10.8 per 1000 population was not appreciably different from the 1970 level of 10.9. figures show a new high for whites of 65,137 deaths while figures for nonwhites dropped slightly from 10,907 to 10,723. Both races showed a small decline in death rate.

Provisional figures show a total of 2,401 infant deaths in 1971. This yielded a record low infant mortality rate of 20.6 per 1000 live births. Both races established new lows, 17.1 for whites and 33.1 for nonwhites. Since 1961 the rate has declined from 23.2 for whites (down 26.3 percent) and from 45.3 for nonwhites (down 26.9 percent.)

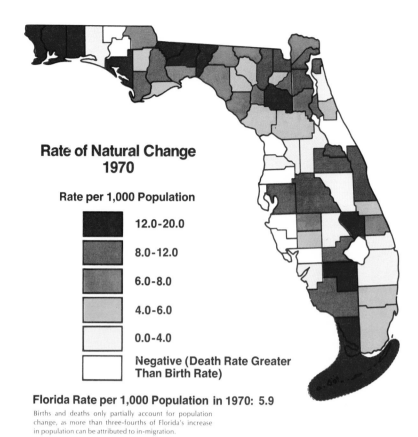

Rate of Natural Change 1970

Rate per 1,000 Population

- 12.0-20.0
- 8.0-12.0
- 6.0-8.0
- 4.0-6.0
- 0.0-4.0
- Negative (Death Rate Greater Than Birth Rate)

Florida Rate per 1,000 Population in 1970: 5.9

Births and deaths only partially account for population change, as more than three-fourths of Florida's increase in population can be attributed to in-migration.

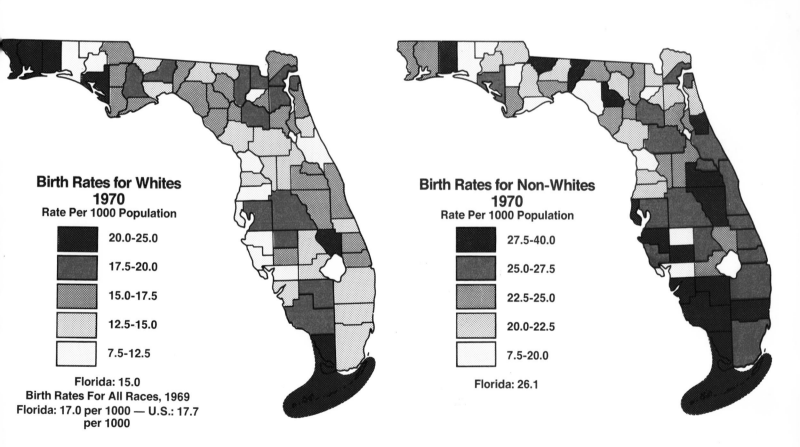

Birth Rates for Whites 1970
Rate Per 1000 Population

- 20.0-25.0
- 17.5-20.0
- 15.0-17.5
- 12.5-15.0
- 7.5-12.5

Florida: 15.0
Birth Rates For All Races, 1969
Florida: 17.0 per 1000 — U.S.: 17.7 per 1000

Birth Rates for Non-Whites 1970
Rate Per 1000 Population

- 27.5-40.0
- 25.0-27.5
- 22.5-25.0
- 20.0-22.5
- 7.5-20.0

Florida: 26.1

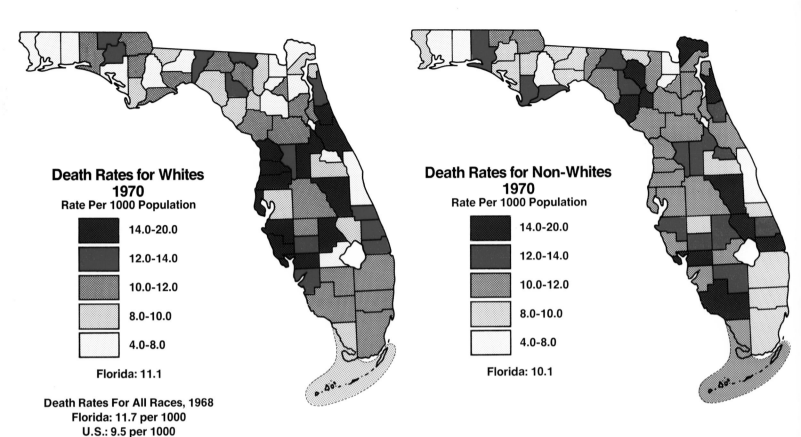

Death Rates for Whites 1970
Rate Per 1000 Population

- ■ 14.0-20.0
- ▨ 12.0-14.0
- ▨ 10.0-12.0
- ▨ 8.0-10.0
- □ 4.0-8.0

Florida: 11.1

Death Rates For All Races, 1968
Florida: 11.7 per 1000
U.S.: 9.5 per 1000

Death Rates for Non-Whites 1970
Rate Per 1000 Population

- ■ 14.0-20.0
- ▨ 12.0-14.0
- ▨ 10.0-12.0
- ▨ 8.0-10.0
- □ 4.0-8.0

Florida: 10.1

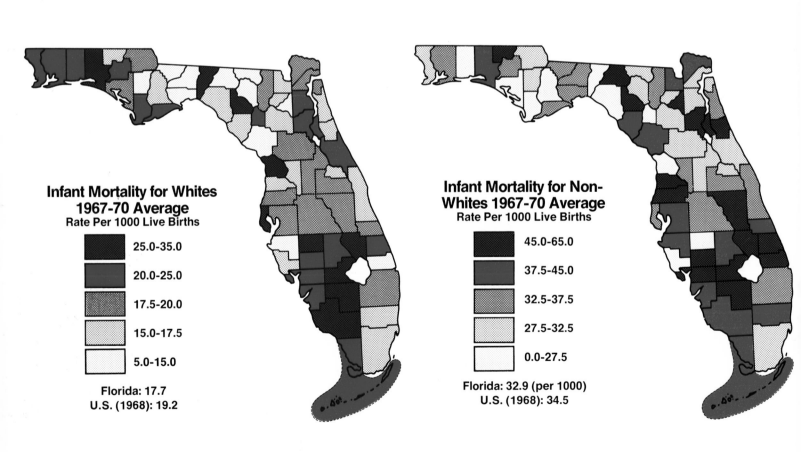

Infant Mortality for Whites 1967-70 Average
Rate Per 1000 Live Births

- ■ 25.0-35.0
- ▨ 20.0-25.0
- ▨ 17.5-20.0
- ▨ 15.0-17.5
- □ 5.0-15.0

Florida: 17.7
U.S. (1968): 19.2

Infant Mortality for Non-Whites 1967-70 Average
Rate Per 1000 Live Births

- ■ 45.0-65.0
- ▨ 37.5-45.0
- ▨ 32.5-37.5
- ▨ 27.5-32.5
- □ 0.0-27.5

Florida: 32.9 (per 1000)
U.S. (1968): 34.5

Florida's and the Nation's Rate of Natural Change, 1917-1970

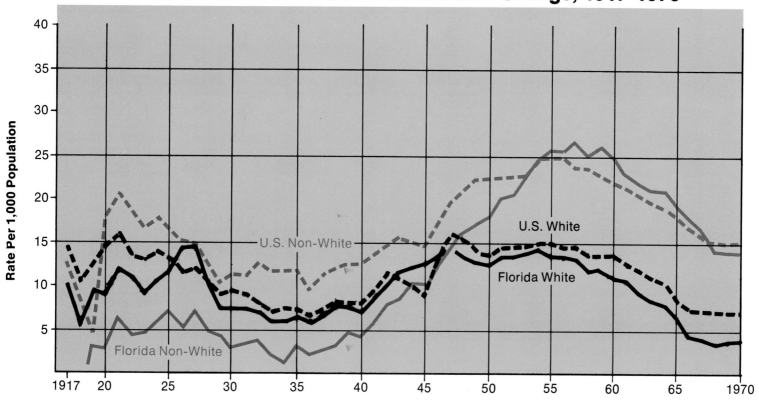

Florida's Birth and Death Rates, 1917-1969

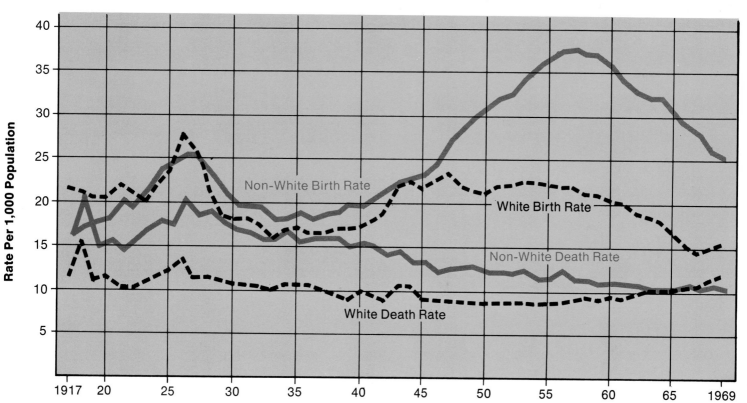

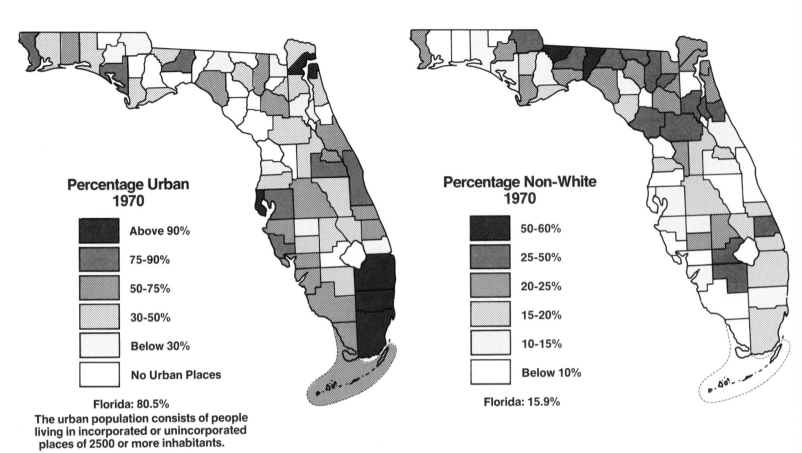

**Percentage Urban
1970**

■ (dark)	Above 90%
■	75-90%
■	50-75%
▦	30-50%
□	Below 30%
□	No Urban Places

Florida: 80.5%
The urban population consists of people
living in incorporated or unincorporated
places of 2500 or more inhabitants.

**Percentage Non-White
1970**

■ (dark)	50-60%
■	25-50%
■	20-25%
▦	15-20%
▨	10-15%
□	Below 10%

Florida: 15.9%

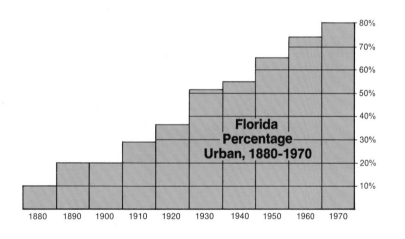

**Florida
Percentage
Urban, 1880-1970**

(graph y-axis: 10% to 80%; x-axis: 1880, 1890, 1900, 1910, 1920, 1930, 1940, 1950, 1960, 1970)

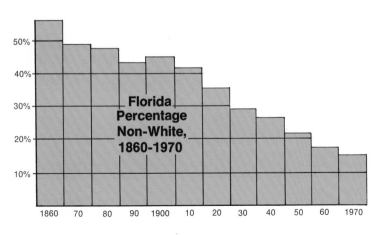

**Florida
Percentage
Non-White,
1860-1970**

(graph y-axis: 10% to 50%; x-axis: 1860, 70, 80, 90, 1900, 10, 20, 30, 40, 50, 60, 1970)

Birthplace of Florida Residents

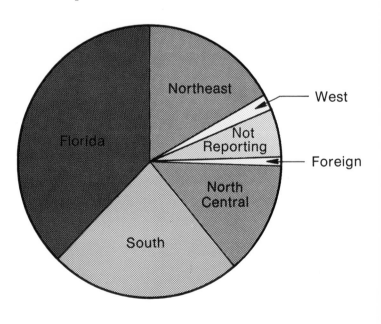

(pie chart labels: Florida, Northeast, West, Not Reporting, Foreign, North Central, South)

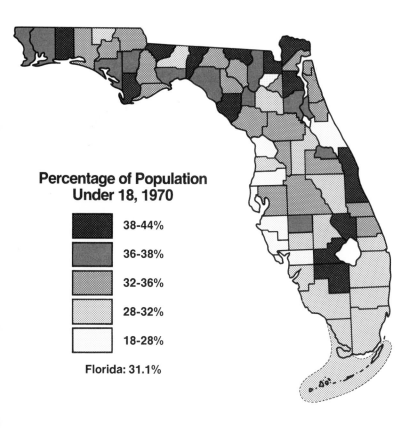

Percentage of Population Under 18, 1970

■	38-44%
▨	36-38%
▨	32-36%
▫	28-32%
□	18-28%

Florida: 31.1%

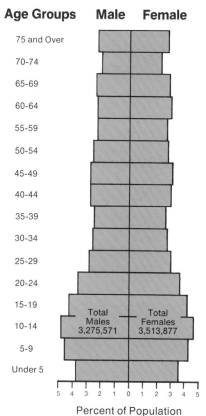

Population Pyramid
Florida, 1970

Age Groups	Male	Female
75 and Over		
70-74		
65-69		
60-64		
55-59		
50-54		
45-49		
40-44		
35-39		
30-34		
25-29		
20-24		
15-19		
10-14	Total Males 3,275,571	Total Females 3,513,877
5-9		
Under 5		

5 4 3 2 1 0 1 2 3 4 5

Percent of Population

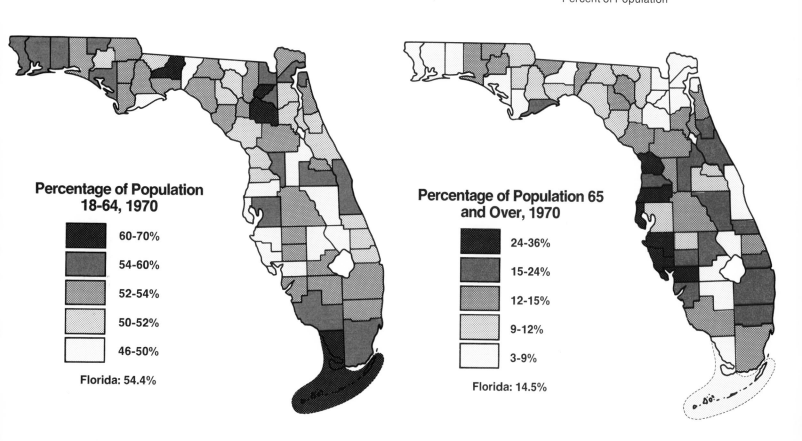

Percentage of Population 18-64, 1970

■	60-70%
▨	54-60%
▨	52-54%
▫	50-52%
□	46-50%

Florida: 54.4%

Percentage of Population 65 and Over, 1970

■	24-36%
▨	15-24%
▨	12-15%
▫	9-12%
□	3-9%

Florida: 14.5%

19

Housing

In 1970, Florida had 2.5 million housing units. The median value of owner occupied structures was $15,000 (U.S. $17,000) and the median number of persons living in the housing was 2.4 (U.S. 2.7). Of the houses occupied the year-round, the median number of rooms was 4.7 (U.S. 5.0) and 5.1 percent of these homes lacked some or all plumbing facilities, compared to the 6.9 percent for the nation.

In 1972, 70 percent of construction in Florida was in residential buildings. The trend in residential construction in the early 70's is to the condominium. The only major area of Florida construction that declined in activity in 1972 was the conventional, single-family home. The general trend in major urban areas was a decline in home building while apartment and condominium units increased rapidly. The high cost of land and construction labor were the two main causes for this trend. In most urban areas in the early 70's new home prices increased at an annual rate of 10 to 15 percent. It was not uncommon for land costs to double in a single year. The average price of a new home in the Miami area was $34,123 in 1972. The high cost of single family residences is also seen in the fact that in 1972 Florida had 282,123 mobile homes, according to the State Department of Highway Safety and Motor Vehicles.

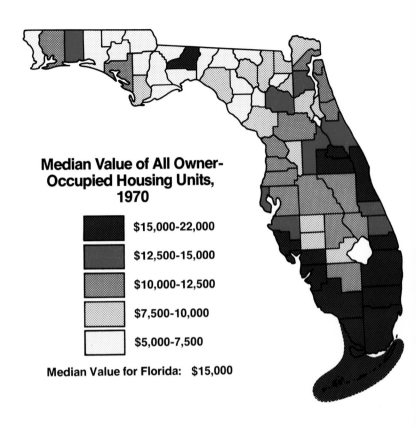

Median Value of All Owner-Occupied Housing Units, 1970

- $15,000-22,000
- $12,500-15,000
- $10,000-12,500
- $7,500-10,000
- $5,000-7,500

Median Value for Florida: $15,000

Townhouses are a new addition to the Florida lifestyle.

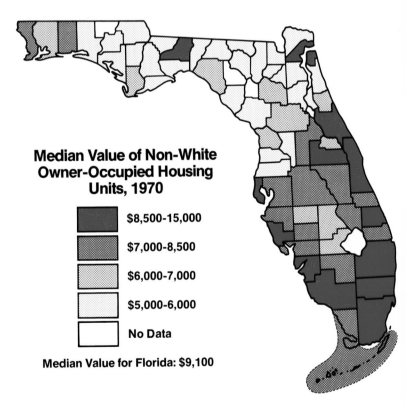

Median Value of Non-White Owner-Occupied Housing Units, 1970

- $8,500-15,000
- $7,000-8,500
- $6,000-7,000
- $5,000-6,000
- No Data

Median Value for Florida: $9,100

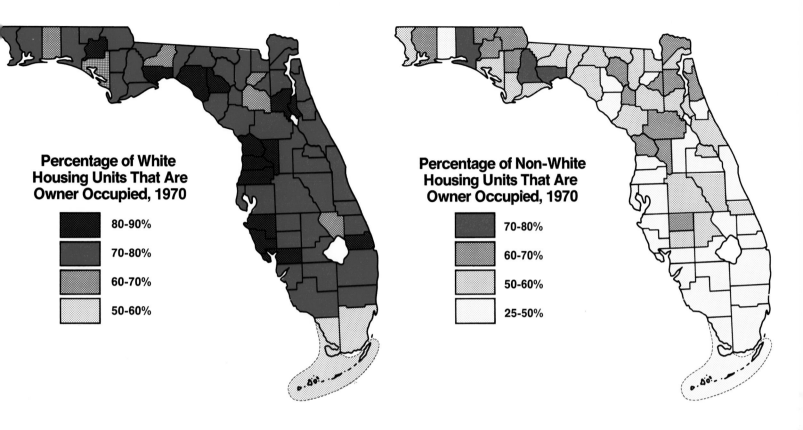

Percentage of White Housing Units That Are Owner Occupied, 1970

- 80-90%
- 70-80%
- 60-70%
- 50-60%

Percentage of Non-White Housing Units That Are Owner Occupied, 1970

- 70-80%
- 60-70%
- 50-60%
- 25-50%

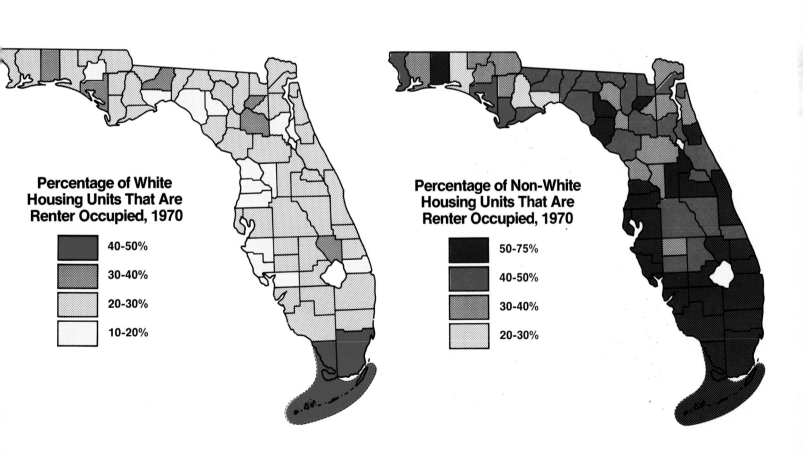

Percentage of White Housing Units That Are Renter Occupied, 1970

- 40-50%
- 30-40%
- 20-30%
- 10-20%

Percentage of Non-White Housing Units That Are Renter Occupied, 1970

- 50-75%
- 40-50%
- 30-40%
- 20-30%

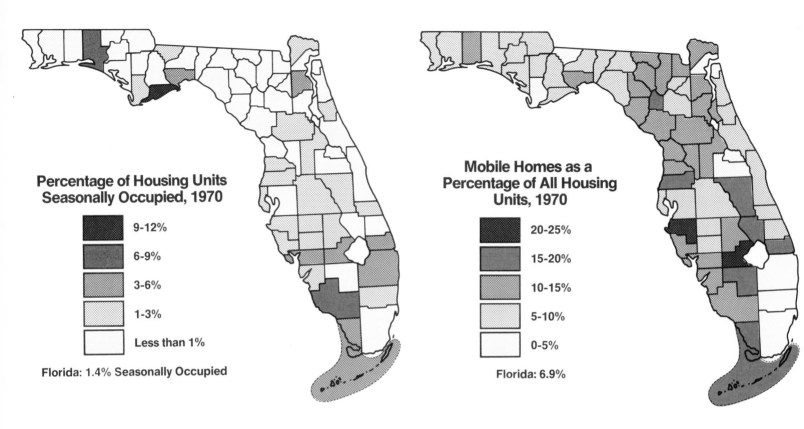

Percentage of Housing Units Seasonally Occupied, 1970

- 9-12%
- 6-9%
- 3-6%
- 1-3%
- Less than 1%

Florida: 1.4% Seasonally Occupied

Mobile Homes as a Percentage of All Housing Units, 1970

- 20-25%
- 15-20%
- 10-15%
- 5-10%
- 0-5%

Florida: 6.9%

Many Florida residents enjoy mobile home living.

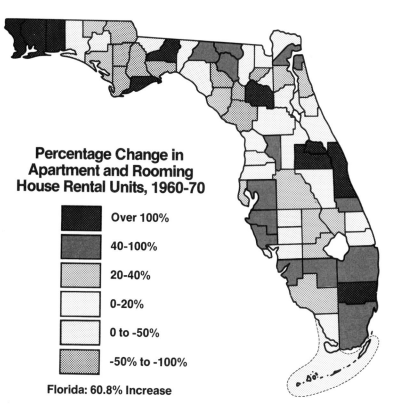

Percentage Change in Apartment and Rooming House Rental Units, 1960-70

- ██ Over 100%
- ▓▓ 40-100%
- ▒▒ 20-40%
- ░░ 0-20%
- □ 0 to -50%
- ▦ -50% to -100%

Florida: 60.8% Increase

Four counties had an exceptionally large increase: Leon (210%), Santa Rosa (348%), Brevard (372%), and Seminole (427%). Liberty, Lafayette, and Union Counties had only a few apartments or rooming houses in 1960 and none in 1970, thus showing 100% decrease.

Condominiums and apartments, Pompano Beach

Median Monthly Rent of Occupied Housing Units 1970

- ██ $81-135
- ▓▓ $66-80
- ▒▒ $51-65
- ░░ $41-50
- □ $30-40

Florida: $93

Persons Per Housing Unit 1970

- ██ 3.6-3.8
- ▓▓ 3.3-3.5
- ▒▒ 3.1-3.2
- ░░ 2.9-3.0
- □ 2.3-2.8

Florida: 2.9

Income

Florida's per capita income in 1971 was $3,930 compared with the United States figure of $4,156. The gap between Florida's per capita income and that of the U.S. in 1971 was $226. This may be compared with a $270 differential in 1960. Two main reasons why Florida does not show stronger gains in per capita income in relation to the U.S. average are: the large number of retirees who pour into the State annually tend to pull down the overall average; and, about 70 percent of the 2.4 million workers in Florida non-farm employment are in retail-wholesale trade, the services, government and/or the real estate-finance fields. These are the lowest paid job sectors. That pattern does not appear to be changing during the 70's.

During 1972 Florida got about 62 new businesses per week, on the average, and more than half of these were in the low pay category. In 1971 the percentage of total income from manufacturing was 8.8 percent while the U.S. figure was 18.7 percent. Within the manufacturing sector the largest group of workers and the largest income figure was from food processing which again is one of the lowest pay categories of manufacturing.

Persons below the poverty level in Florida make up a significant portion of the population. Poverty is used here as defined in the 1970 U.S. Census. It is based on factors such as family size, sex of the family head, number of children under 18 years of age, and farm and nonfarm residence. Of all Floridians in 1969, 16.4% were below the poverty level. A critical fact is that 24.3% of Florida's citizens over 65 fall below the poverty income level.

Of personal income sources in Florida in 1971 wages and salaries led all others with $17 billion dollars while the second biggest single source of income was property, followed by government, which was in turn followed by retail and wholesale trades. While there are many similarities in the pattern of sources of personal income between Florida and the nation the major difference remains the disparity between the impact of manufacturing at each level. Despite steady increases in its manufacturing base over the past two decades, Florida in the 70's is not likely to reach the per capita income average of the nation.

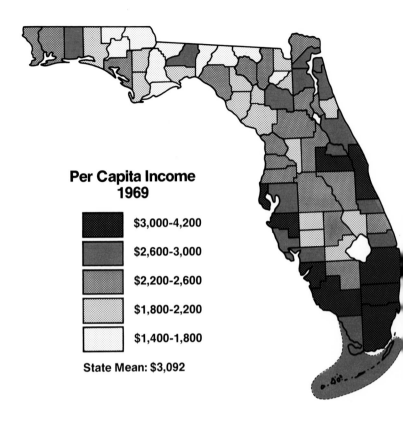

Per Capita Income 1969

$3,000-4,200

$2,600-3,000

$2,200-2,600

$1,800-2,200

$1,400-1,800

State Mean: $3,092

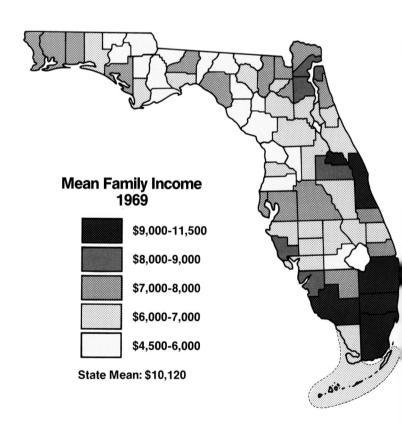

Mean Family Income 1969

$9,000-11,500

$8,000-9,000

$7,000-8,000

$6,000-7,000

$4,500-6,000

State Mean: $10,120

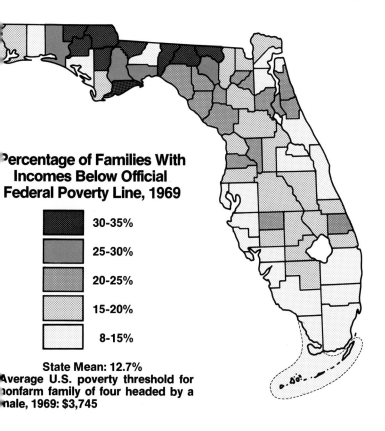

Percentage of Families With Incomes Below Official Federal Poverty Line, 1969

- ■ 30-35%
- ▨ 25-30%
- ▨ 20-25%
- ▨ 15-20%
- □ 8-15%

State Mean: 12.7%
Average U.S. poverty threshold for nonfarm family of four headed by a male, 1969: $3,745

Molten steel for Florida manufacturers

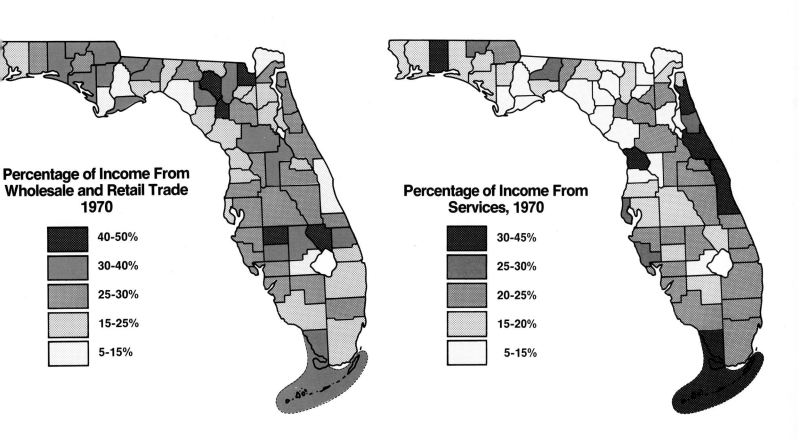

Percentage of Income From Wholesale and Retail Trade 1970

- ■ 40-50%
- ▨ 30-40%
- ▨ 25-30%
- ▨ 15-25%
- □ 5-15%

Percentage of Income From Services, 1970

- ■ 30-45%
- ▨ 25-30%
- ▨ 20-25%
- ▨ 15-20%
- □ 5-15%

Phosphate mine, Polk County

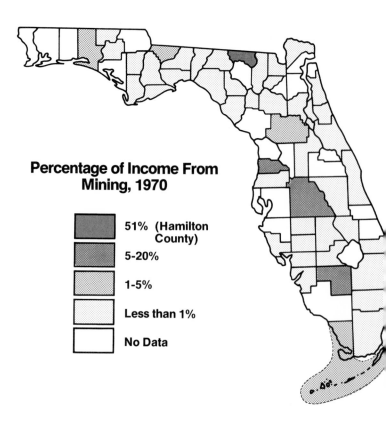

Percentage of Income From Mining, 1970

- 51% (Hamilton County)
- 5-20%
- 1-5%
- Less than 1%
- No Data

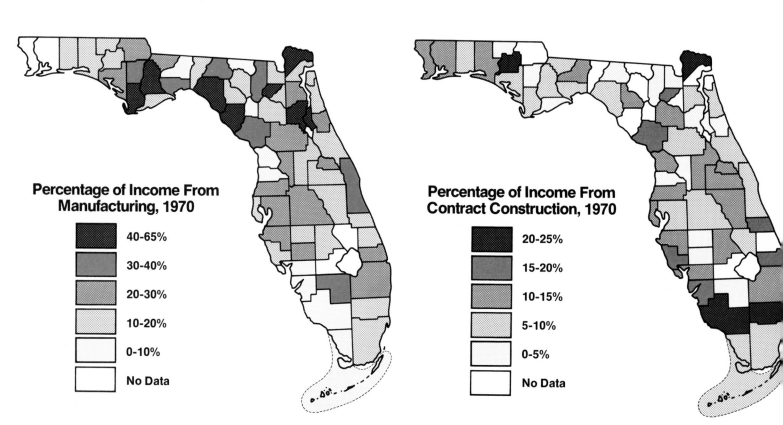

Percentage of Income From Manufacturing, 1970

- 40-65%
- 30-40%
- 20-30%
- 10-20%
- 0-10%
- No Data

Percentage of Income From Contract Construction, 1970

- 20-25%
- 15-20%
- 10-15%
- 5-10%
- 0-5%
- No Data

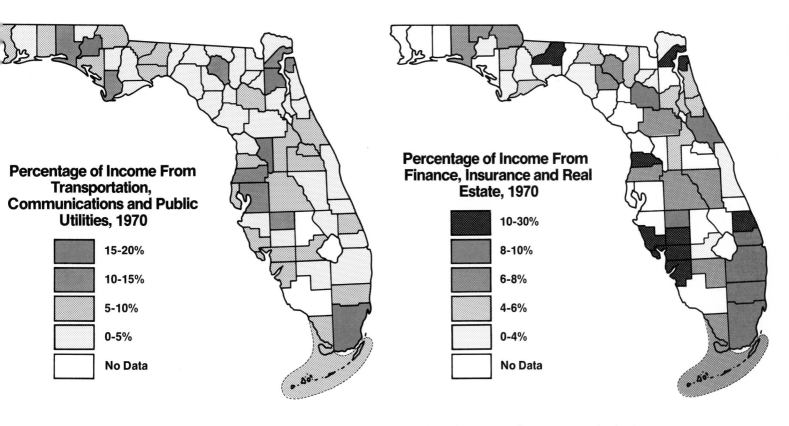

Percentage of Income From Transportation, Communications and Public Utilities, 1970

- 15-20%
- 10-15%
- 5-10%
- 0-5%
- No Data

Percentage of Income From Finance, Insurance and Real Estate, 1970

- 10-30%
- 8-10%
- 6-8%
- 4-6%
- 0-4%
- No Data

Values for Hernando (28.7%) and Charlotte (26.4%) counties far exceed the value for Lee (12.8%), the next highest county.

Total Private Nonfarm Earnings, 1970

Manufacturing	Mining	Construction	Transportation Communications Public Utilities	Wholesale and Retail Trades	Finance Insurance Real Estate	Services	Others
18.4%	0.5%	11.6%	10.5%	25.5%	8.7%	24.0%	0.9%

Education

Florida's Constitution grants free education to all students and instructs the legislature to provide a liberal maintenance. In 1973, the legislature adopted a Full Time Equivalent Student formula which returns state monies to the counties on the basis of the number of students in a school system. It also provides a major shift of responsibility from the state to the local school districts.

In 1970, 1.7 million students were enrolled in both public and private schools in the state of Florida. In 1970, of all Floridians 25 years old and over the median school years completed was 12.1.

All public schools are directed and controlled at the county level by a county school board. The chief officer is the county Superintendent of Public Instruction. In some counties the superintendent is elected while in other counties he is appointed.

Data for the 1971-72 school year show that in Florida's public schools there was an enrollment of 1,608,659, of whom 78,572 graduated from high school. The average salary of teachers and other instructional staff in the 1971-72 school year was $9,434.

Of the 262 public high schools with graduating classes in 1972, only 14 had 25 or fewer graduates. Over 87% of the high school seniors came from schools with more than 200 pupils in the graduating class. A total of 49.2% of these graduates entered college during the 1973 school year and an additional 3.72% entered technical, trade, or other types of formal training. Of the 38,658 graduates of 1972 who entered college 59% entered junior colleges, 26% entered universities within the State and 15% entered out of state universities.

Florida's 9 institutions of higher learning are administered by the Board of Regents, a policy making body under the Department of Education. Members of the Board of Regents, 9 in number, are appointed by the Governor to staggered 9 year terms. Florida's 27 public community and junior colleges are administered by the Division of Community Colleges under the State Department of Education.

Public Education Dollar by Legislative Appropriations 1972-73

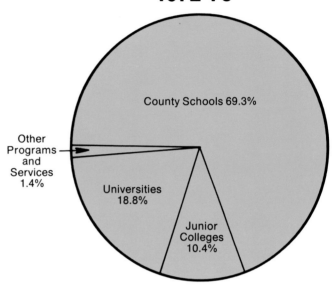

Division of Public University Appropriations 1972-73

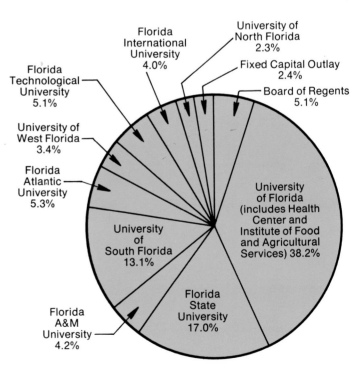

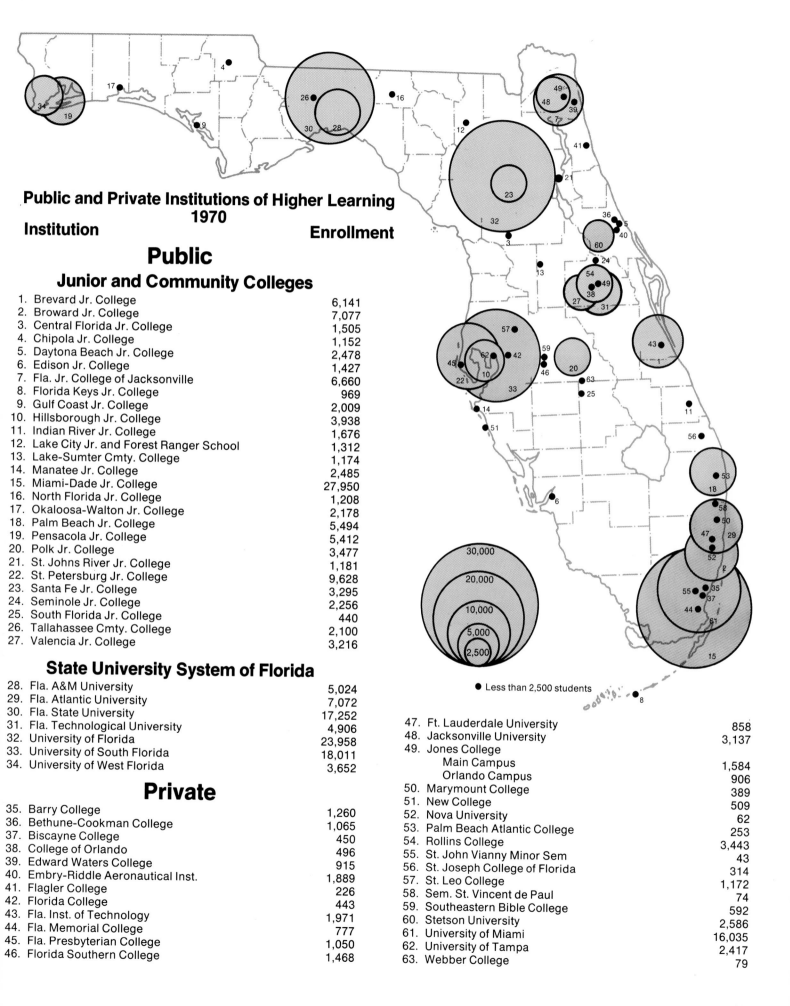

Public and Private Institutions of Higher Learning
1970

Institution	Enrollment

Public
Junior and Community Colleges

1. Brevard Jr. College	6,141
2. Broward Jr. College	7,077
3. Central Florida Jr. College	1,505
4. Chipola Jr. College	1,152
5. Daytona Beach Jr. College	2,478
6. Edison Jr. College	1,427
7. Fla. Jr. College of Jacksonville	6,660
8. Florida Keys Jr. College	969
9. Gulf Coast Jr. College	2,009
10. Hillsborough Jr. College	3,938
11. Indian River Jr. College	1,676
12. Lake City Jr. and Forest Ranger School	1,312
13. Lake-Sumter Cmty. College	1,174
14. Manatee Jr. College	2,485
15. Miami-Dade Jr. College	27,950
16. North Florida Jr. College	1,208
17. Okaloosa-Walton Jr. College	2,178
18. Palm Beach Jr. College	5,494
19. Pensacola Jr. College	5,412
20. Polk Jr. College	3,477
21. St. Johns River Jr. College	1,181
22. St. Petersburg Jr. College	9,628
23. Santa Fe Jr. College	3,295
24. Seminole Jr. College	2,256
25. South Florida Jr. College	440
26. Tallahassee Cmty. College	2,100
27. Valencia Jr. College	3,216

State University System of Florida

28. Fla. A&M University	5,024
29. Fla. Atlantic University	7,072
30. Fla. State University	17,252
31. Fla. Technological University	4,906
32. University of Florida	23,958
33. University of South Florida	18,011
34. University of West Florida	3,652

Private

35. Barry College	1,260
36. Bethune-Cookman College	1,065
37. Biscayne College	450
38. College of Orlando	496
39. Edward Waters College	915
40. Embry-Riddle Aeronautical Inst.	1,889
41. Flagler College	226
42. Florida College	443
43. Fla. Inst. of Technology	1,971
44. Fla. Memorial College	777
45. Fla. Presbyterian College	1,050
46. Florida Southern College	1,468
47. Ft. Lauderdale University	858
48. Jacksonville University	3,137
49. Jones College	
Main Campus	1,584
Orlando Campus	906
50. Marymount College	389
51. New College	509
52. Nova University	62
53. Palm Beach Atlantic College	253
54. Rollins College	3,443
55. St. John Vianny Minor Sem	43
56. St. Joseph College of Florida	314
57. St. Leo College	1,172
58. Sem. St. Vincent de Paul	74
59. Southeastern Bible College	592
60. Stetson University	2,586
61. University of Miami	16,035
62. University of Tampa	2,417
63. Webber College	79

• Less than 2,500 students

30,000
20,000
10,000
5,000
2,500

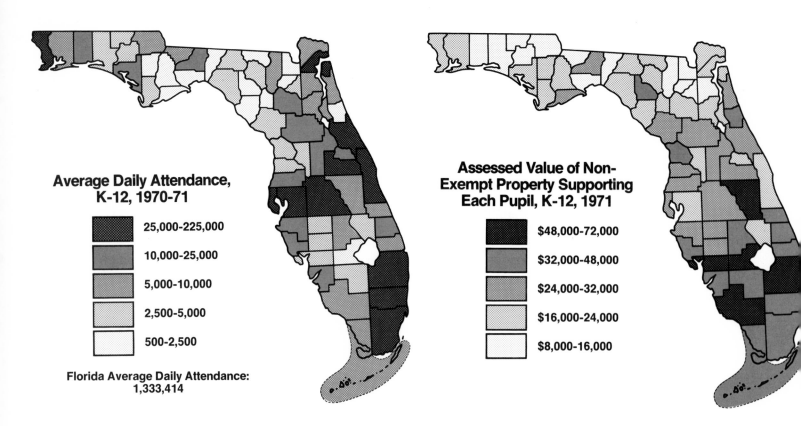

Average Daily Attendance, K-12, 1970-71

■	25,000-225,000
▨	10,000-25,000
▨	5,000-10,000
▨	2,500-5,000
□	500-2,500

Florida Average Daily Attendance: 1,333,414

Assessed Value of Non-Exempt Property Supporting Each Pupil, K-12, 1971

■	$48,000-72,000
▨	$32,000-48,000
▨	$24,000-32,000
▨	$16,000-24,000
□	$8,000-16,000

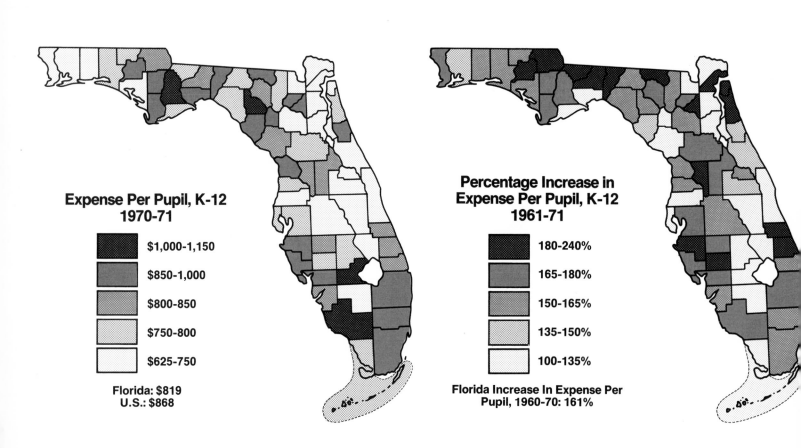

Expense Per Pupil, K-12 1970-71

■	$1,000-1,150
▨	$850-1,000
▨	$800-850
▨	$750-800
□	$625-750

**Florida: $819
U.S.: $868**

Percentage Increase in Expense Per Pupil, K-12 1961-71

■	180-240%
▨	165-180%
▨	150-165%
▨	135-150%
□	100-135%

Florida Increase In Expense Per Pupil, 1960-70: 161%

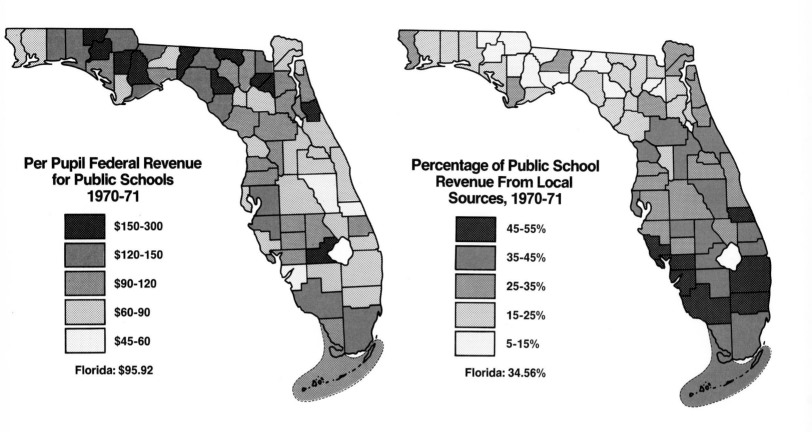

**Per Pupil Federal Revenue
for Public Schools
1970-71**

■	$150-300
■	$120-150
■	$90-120
▢	$60-90
□	$45-60

Florida: $95.92

**Percentage of Public School
Revenue From Local
Sources, 1970-71**

■	45-55%
■	35-45%
■	25-35%
▢	15-25%
□	5-15%

Florida: 34.56%

Sources of Revenue for Education

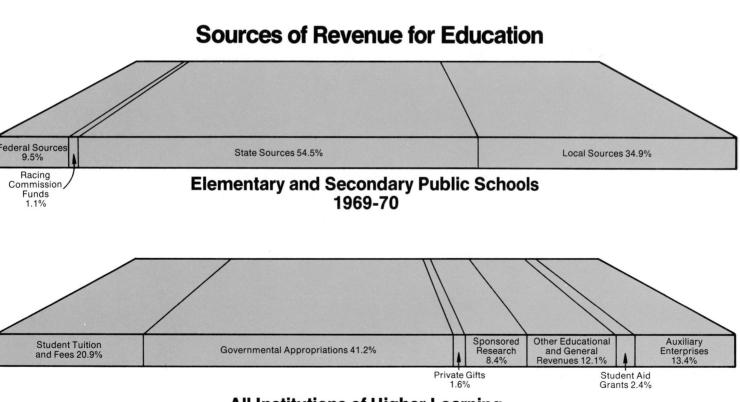

Federal Sources 9.5%

Racing Commission Funds 1.1%

State Sources 54.5%

Local Sources 34.9%

**Elementary and Secondary Public Schools
1969-70**

Student Tuition and Fees 20.9%

Governmental Appropriations 41.2%

Private Gifts 1.6%

Sponsored Research 8.4%

Other Educational and General Revenues 12.1%

Student Aid Grants 2.4%

Auxiliary Enterprises 13.4%

**All Institutions of Higher Learning
1968-69**

Teachers' Salaries

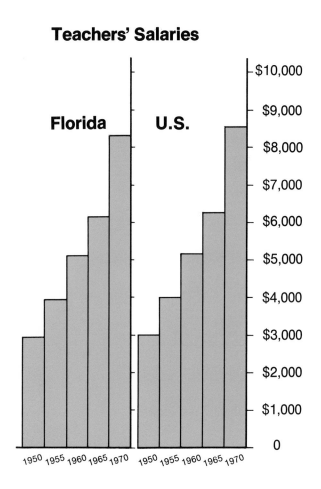

Florida   U.S.

1950 1955 1960 1965 1970   1950 1955 1960 1965 1970

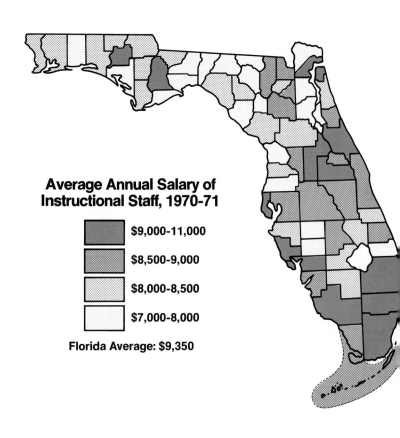

Average Annual Salary of Instructional Staff, 1970-71

- $9,000-11,000
- $8,500-9,000
- $8,000-8,500
- $7,000-8,000

Florida Average: $9,350

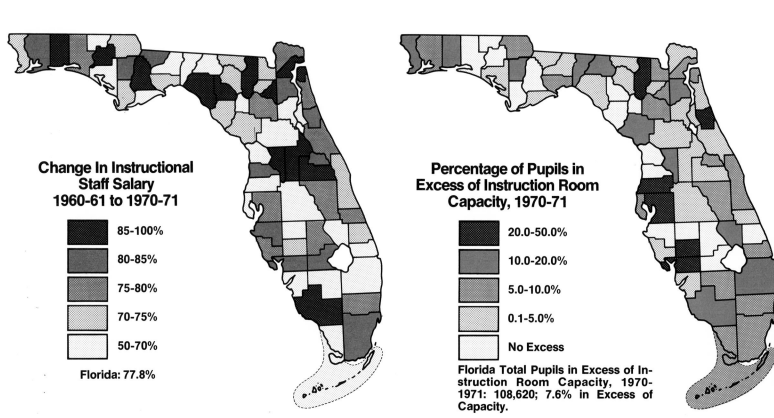

Change In Instructional Staff Salary 1960-61 to 1970-71

- 85-100%
- 80-85%
- 75-80%
- 70-75%
- 50-70%

Florida: 77.8%

Percentage of Pupils in Excess of Instruction Room Capacity, 1970-71

- 20.0-50.0%
- 10.0-20.0%
- 5.0-10.0%
- 0.1-5.0%
- No Excess

Florida Total Pupils in Excess of Instruction Room Capacity, 1970-1971: 108,620; 7.6% in Excess of Capacity.

Median School Years Completed for Persons 25 Years Old and Over
1970

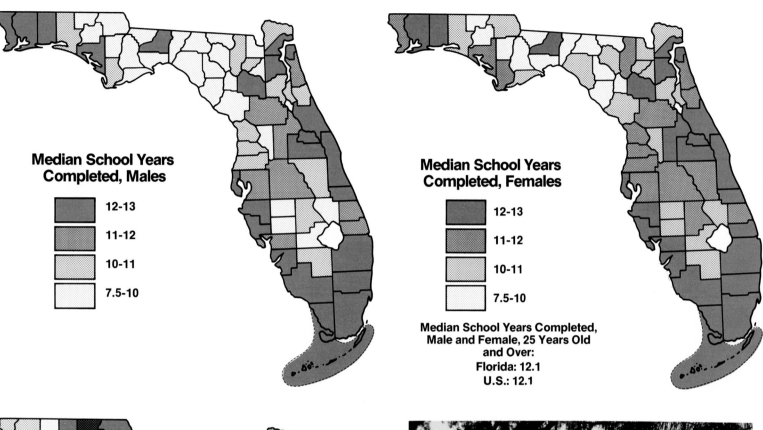

Median School Years Completed, Males

▨	12-13
▨	11-12
░	10-11
□	7.5-10

Median School Years Completed, Females

▨	12-13
▨	11-12
░	10-11
□	7.5-10

Median School Years Completed, Male and Female, 25 Years Old and Over:
Florida: 12.1
U.S.: 12.1

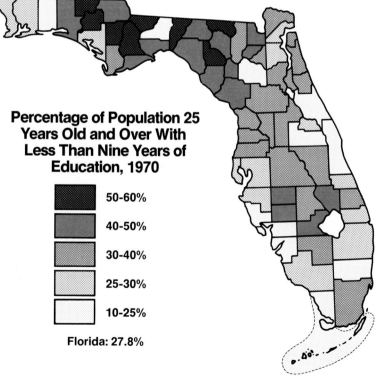

Percentage of Population 25 Years Old and Over With Less Than Nine Years of Education, 1970

▰	50-60%
▨	40-50%
▨	30-40%
░	25-30%
□	10-25%

Florida: 27.8%

University of Tampa's main building

33

Government and Politics

Florida's government is a representative government led by a governor, a seven-member cabinet, a two house legislature, and a supreme court. There are approximately 450 different governmental units in Florida, including about 385 municipal, 67 county, and the state government.

The governor is the chief executive officer for the state of Florida. His executive branch is the chief law administering and law enforcement department of the State. The 1968 Florida constitution allows the governor to hold office for only two successive terms. The 1968 Florida constitution instructs the legislature to apportion itself into not less than 30 nor more than 40 consecutively numbered senatorial districts, and into not less than 80 nor more than 120 consecutively numbered representative districts. Both houses accepted the maximum number. This apportioning, which means to politically divide the state into equal population areas for representation, takes place the second year after each decennial (ten year) census. Florida is represented in the U.S. Congress by 15 congressmen and 2 senators.

The power to make laws is equally shared by the Florida Senate and the House of Representatives. Any type of legislation may be introduced in either house. Both the Senate and the House of Representatives must give their approval of any bill before it may be sent to the governor for his approval or veto. This dual system is called a bi-cameral, or two-chamber legislature. Some citizens have expressed their desire to change Florida's legislature into a uni-cameral, or one house legislature. The one house system can be more efficient; however, it does not have the checks and balances characteristics possessed by the bi-cameral legislature.

The State Supreme Court has seven justices elected for six year terms. Within certain limits this court is the final court of appeal and makes the rulings upon questions of constitutionality. The district courts of appeal hear appeals in certain cases so as to relieve the burden of the Supreme Court. Circuit courts are set up to have jurisdiction over cases in equity, tax legality, title cases, and cases beyond the jurisdiction of inferior courts. Florida is a part of the fifth judicial circuit of the Federal court system.

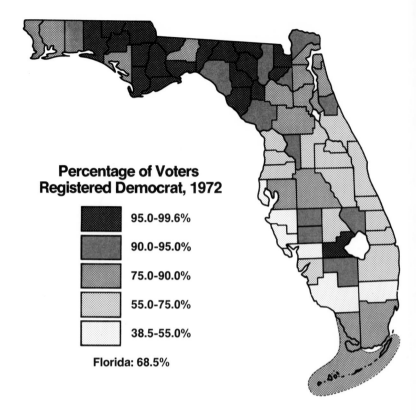

Percentage of Voters Registered Democrat, 1972

95.0-99.6%

90.0-95.0%

75.0-90.0%

55.0-75.0%

38.5-55.0%

Florida: 68.5%

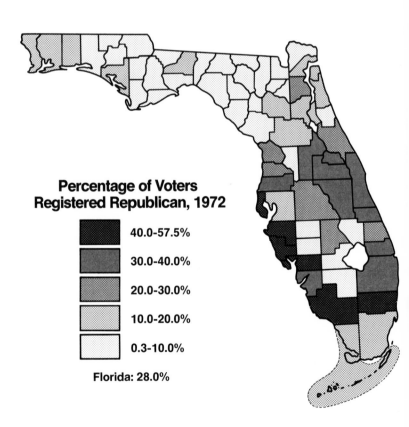

Percentage of Voters Registered Republican, 1972

40.0-57.5%

30.0-40.0%

20.0-30.0%

10.0-20.0%

0.3-10.0%

Florida: 28.0%

Registered Voters, 1972

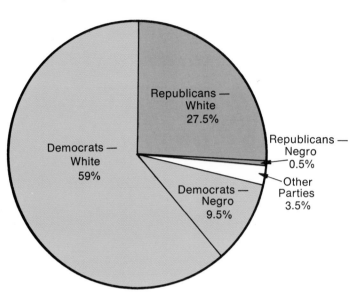

Democrats —
White
59%

Republicans —
White
27.5%

Republicans —
Negro
0.5%

Other
Parties
3.5%

Democrats —
Negro
9.5%

Figures are nearest one-half percent.

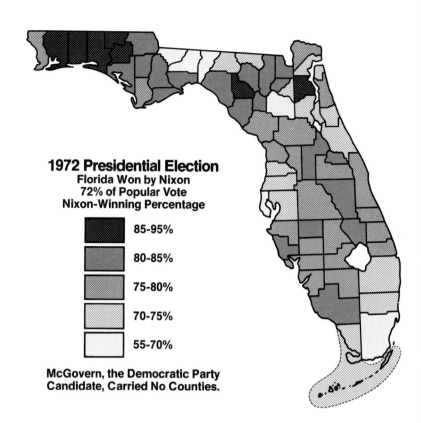

1972 Presidential Election
Florida Won by Nixon
72% of Popular Vote
Nixon-Winning Percentage

	85-95%
	80-85%
	75-80%
	70-75%
	55-70%

**McGovern, the Democratic Party
Candidate, Carried No Counties.**

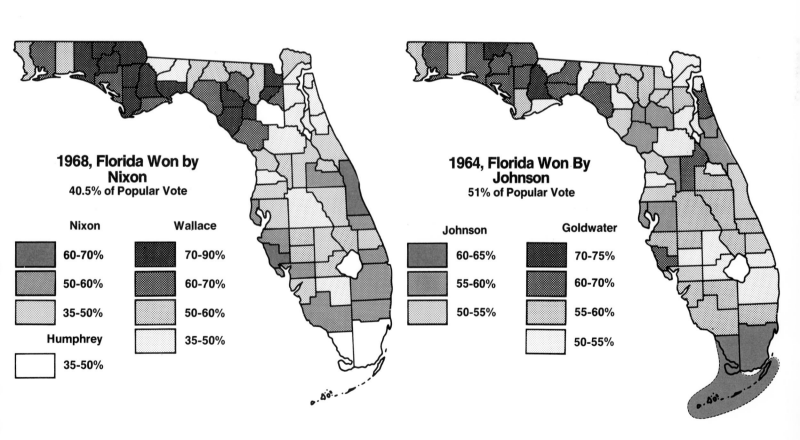

**1968, Florida Won by
Nixon**
40.5% of Popular Vote

Nixon		Wallace	
	60-70%		70-90%
	50-60%		60-70%
	35-50%		50-60%
Humphrey			35-50%
	35-50%		

**1964, Florida Won By
Johnson**
51% of Popular Vote

Johnson		Goldwater	
	60-65%		70-75%
	55-60%		60-70%
	50-55%		55-60%
			50-55%

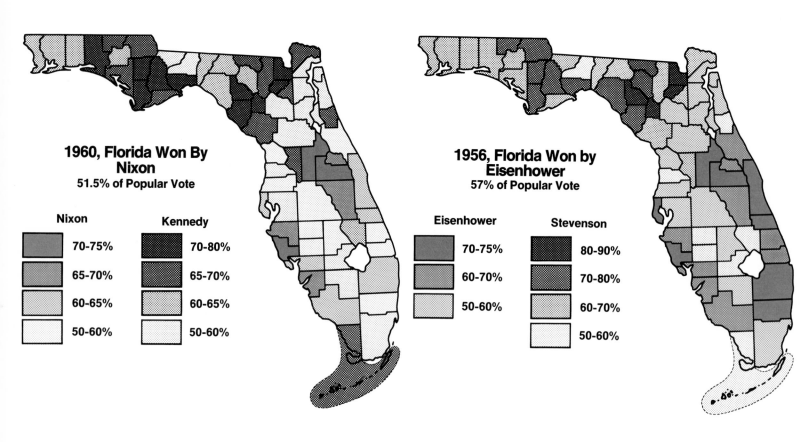

1960, Florida Won By Nixon
51.5% of Popular Vote

Nixon		Kennedy	
	70-75%		70-80%
	65-70%		65-70%
	60-65%		60-65%
	50-60%		50-60%

1956, Florida Won by Eisenhower
57% of Popular Vote

Eisenhower		Stevenson	
	70-75%		80-90%
	60-70%		70-80%
	50-60%		60-70%
			50-60%

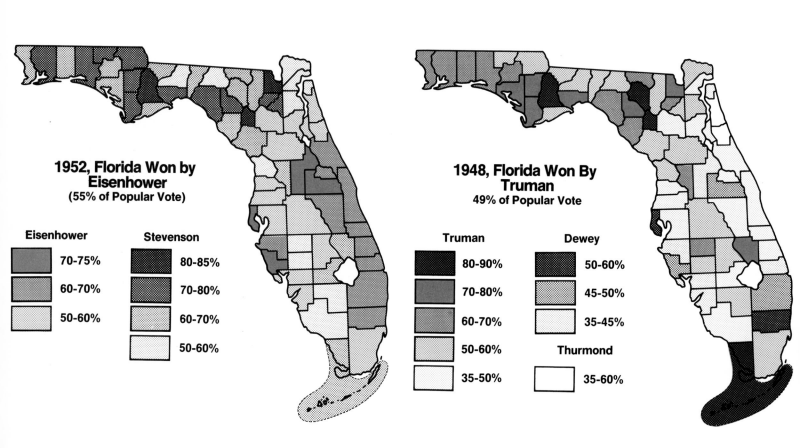

1952, Florida Won by Eisenhower
(55% of Popular Vote)

Eisenhower		Stevenson	
	70-75%		80-85%
	60-70%		70-80%
	50-60%		60-70%
			50-60%

1948, Florida Won By Truman
49% of Popular Vote

Truman		Dewey	
	80-90%		50-60%
	70-80%		45-50%
	60-70%		35-45%
	50-60%	**Thurmond**	
	35-50%		35-60%

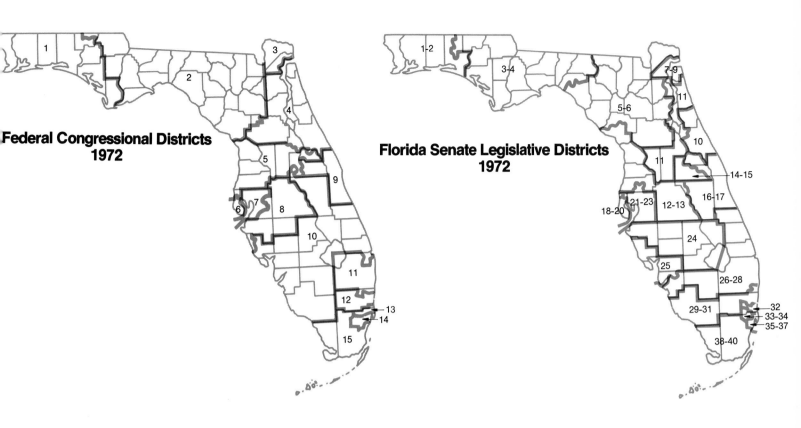

Federal Congressional Districts 1972

Florida Senate Legislative Districts 1972

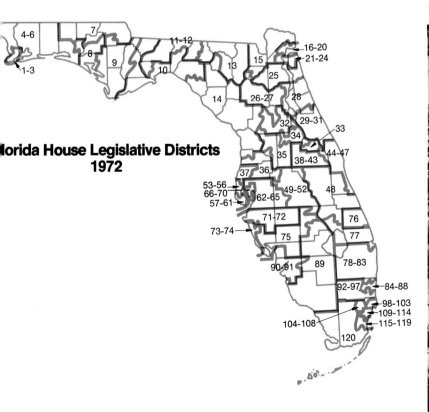

Florida House Legislative Districts 1972

Senate legislative chamber, Tallahassee

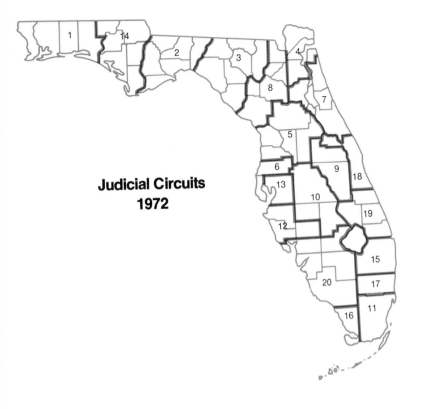

**Judicial Circuits
1972**

Supreme Court Building, Tallahassee

**Federal Court Districts
1972**

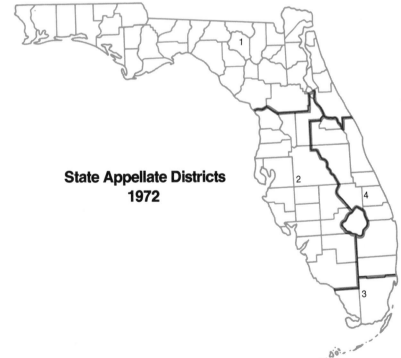

**State Appellate Districts
1972**

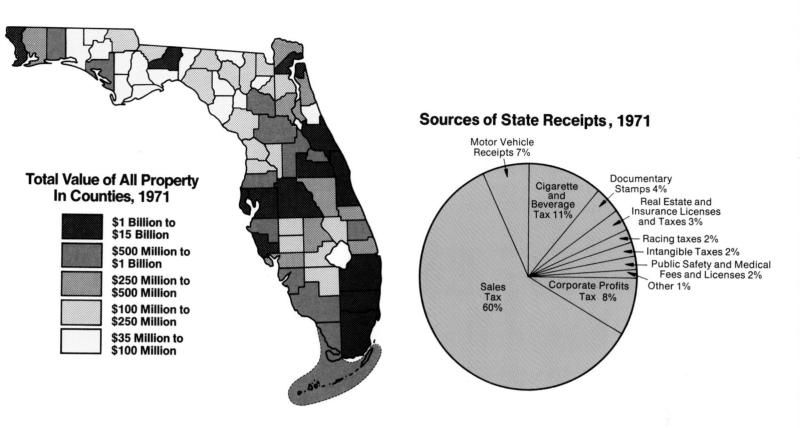

Total Value of All Property In Counties, 1971

- $1 Billion to $15 Billion
- $500 Million to $1 Billion
- $250 Million to $500 Million
- $100 Million to $250 Million
- $35 Million to $100 Million

Sources of State Receipts, 1971

- Motor Vehicle Receipts 7%
- Cigarette and Beverage Tax 11%
- Documentary Stamps 4%
- Real Estate and Insurance Licenses and Taxes 3%
- Racing taxes 2%
- Intangible Taxes 2%
- Public Safety and Medical Fees and Licenses 2%
- Other 1%
- Sales Tax 60%
- Corporate Profits Tax 8%

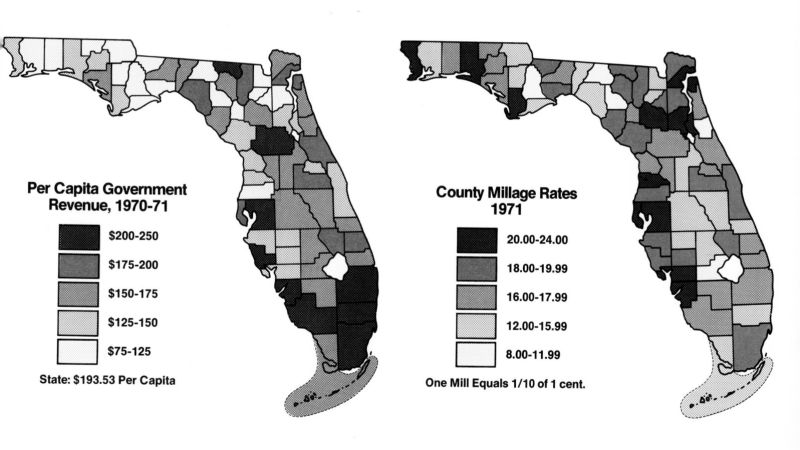

Per Capita Government Revenue, 1970-71

- $200-250
- $175-200
- $150-175
- $125-150
- $75-125

State: $193.53 Per Capita

County Millage Rates 1971

- 20.00-24.00
- 18.00-19.99
- 16.00-17.99
- 12.00-15.99
- 8.00-11.99

One Mill Equals 1/10 of 1 cent.

39

Capitol Building, Tallahassee

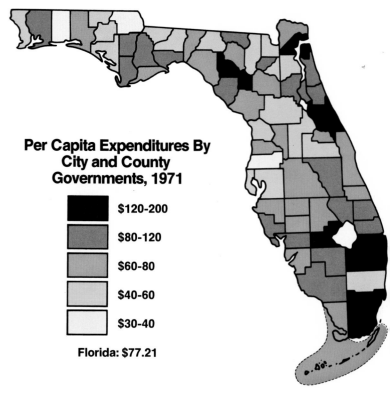

**Per Capita Expenditures By
City and County
Governments, 1971**

■	**$120-200**
■	**$80-120**
■	**$60-80**
■	**$40-60**
□	**$30-40**

Florida: $77.21

**Expenditures of the Florida Tax Dollar
From the General Revenue Fund
1971-1972**

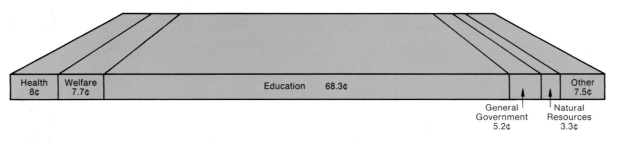

Health 8¢ | Welfare 7.7¢ | Education 68.3¢ | General Government 5.2¢ | Natural Resources 3.3¢ | Other 7.5¢

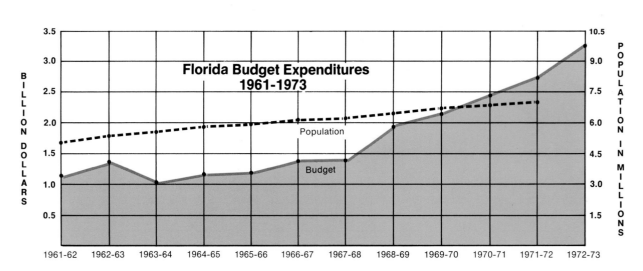

**Florida Budget Expenditures
1961-1973**

Physical Characteristics

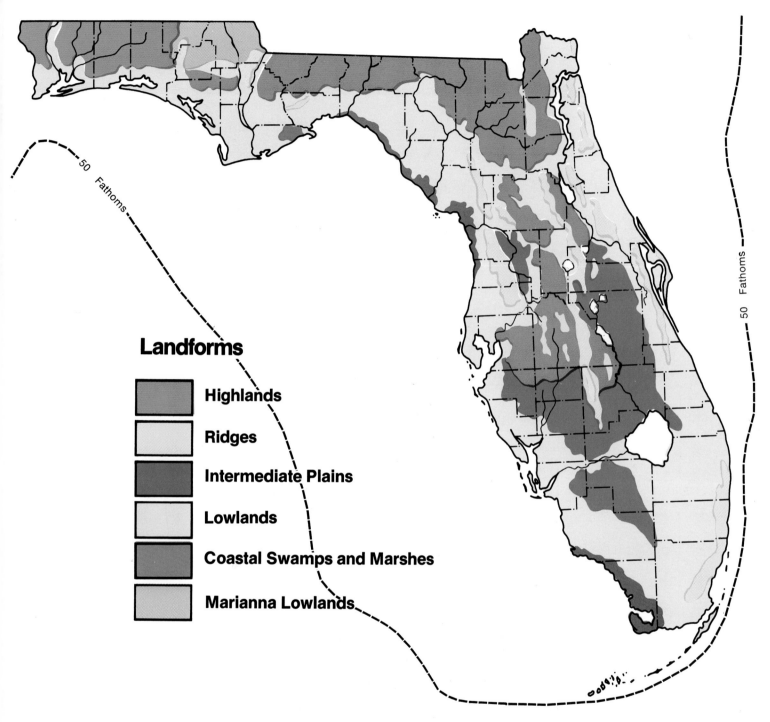

Landforms

- Highlands
- Ridges
- Intermediate Plains
- Lowlands
- Coastal Swamps and Marshes
- Marianna Lowlands

Florida is the second largest state in area east of the Mississippi River. Its 58,560 square miles is considerably larger than a number of nations in the world. For example Portugal and Austria are smaller and the combined areas of Belgium, the Netherlands, and Luxembourg are smaller than Florida. Florida extends from 24 degrees 31 minutes N to 31 degrees N latitude. Its east-west extent is from 80 degrees West longitude to 87 degrees 35 minutes West longitude.

Relationships among Florida's location and physical characteristics are very important. For example, Florida's sub-tropical climate is influenced by the marine character of its shape, its latitude, and the fact that the relief of its land forms is very slight. Florida's numerous inland lakes and wetlands modify many local micro-climates. Florida's climate, vegetation and bedrock provide Florida with a sandy, acid, infertile soil that is low in humus.

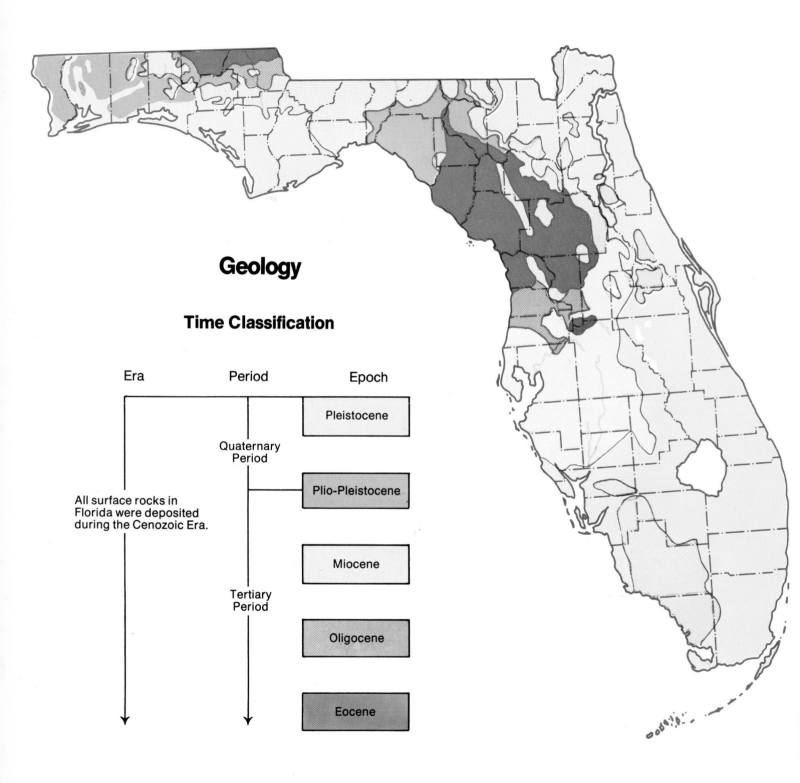

Geology

Time Classification

Era	Period	Epoch

All surface rocks in Florida were deposited during the Cenozoic Era.

Quaternary Period
- Pleistocene
- Plio-Pleistocene

Tertiary Period
- Miocene
- Oligocene
- Eocene

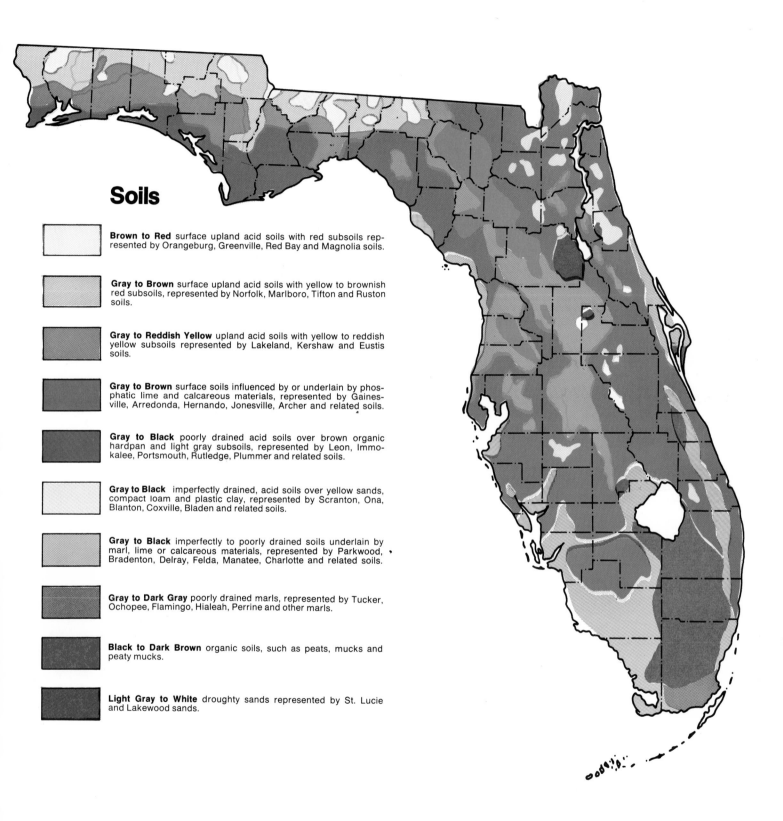

Soils

Brown to Red surface upland acid soils with red subsoils represented by Orangeburg, Greenville, Red Bay and Magnolia soils.

Gray to Brown surface upland acid soils with yellow to brownish red subsoils, represented by Norfolk, Marlboro, Tifton and Ruston soils.

Gray to Reddish Yellow upland acid soils with yellow to reddish yellow subsoils represented by Lakeland, Kershaw and Eustis soils.

Gray to Brown surface soils influenced by or underlain by phosphatic lime and calcareous materials, represented by Gainesville, Arredonda, Hernando, Jonesville, Archer and related soils.

Gray to Black poorly drained acid soils over brown organic hardpan and light gray subsoils, represented by Leon, Immokalee, Portsmouth, Rutledge, Plummer and related soils.

Gray to Black imperfectly drained, acid soils over yellow sands, compact loam and plastic clay, represented by Scranton, Ona, Blanton, Coxville, Bladen and related soils.

Gray to Black imperfectly to poorly drained soils underlain by marl, lime or calcareous materials, represented by Parkwood, Bradenton, Delray, Felda, Manatee, Charlotte and related soils.

Gray to Dark Gray poorly drained marls, represented by Tucker, Ochopee, Flamingo, Hialeah, Perrine and other marls.

Black to Dark Brown organic soils, such as peats, mucks and peaty mucks.

Light Gray to White droughty sands represented by St. Lucie and Lakewood sands.

Natural Vegetation

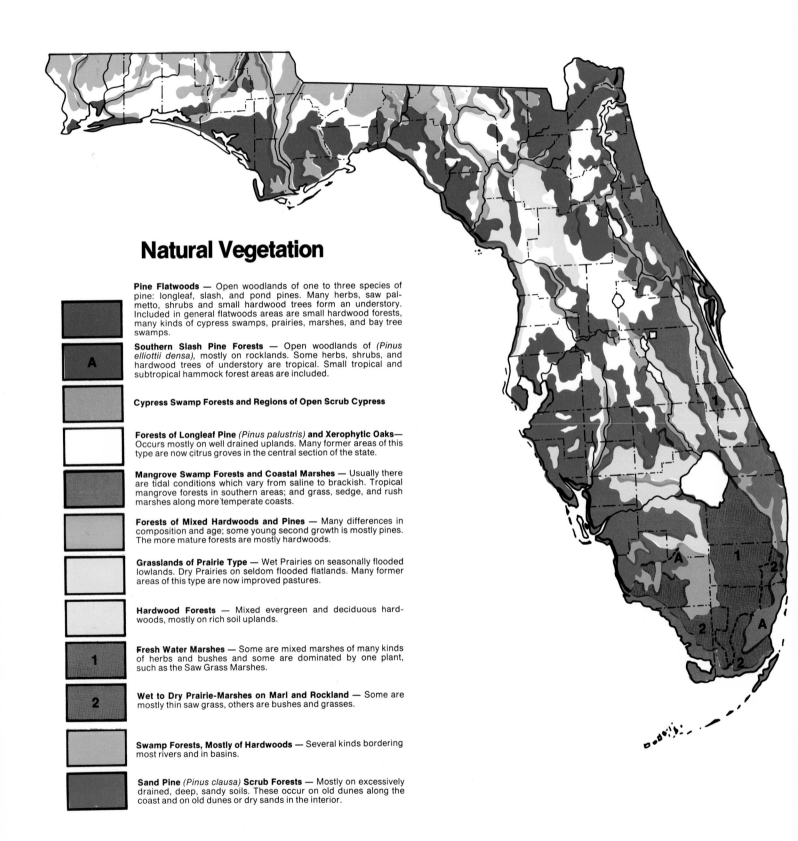

Pine Flatwoods — Open woodlands of one to three species of pine: longleaf, slash, and pond pines. Many herbs, saw palmetto, shrubs and small hardwood trees form an understory. Included in general flatwoods areas are small hardwood forests, many kinds of cypress swamps, prairies, marshes, and bay tree swamps.

Southern Slash Pine Forests — Open woodlands of *(Pinus elliottii densa)*, mostly on rocklands. Some herbs, shrubs, and hardwood trees of understory are tropical. Small tropical and subtropical hammock forest areas are included.

Cypress Swamp Forests and Regions of Open Scrub Cypress

Forests of Longleaf Pine *(Pinus palustris)* **and Xerophytic Oaks**— Occurs mostly on well drained uplands. Many former areas of this type are now citrus groves in the central section of the state.

Mangrove Swamp Forests and Coastal Marshes — Usually there are tidal conditions which vary from saline to brackish. Tropical mangrove forests in southern areas; and grass, sedge, and rush marshes along more temperate coasts.

Forests of Mixed Hardwoods and Pines — Many differences in composition and age; some young second growth is mostly pines. The more mature forests are mostly hardwoods.

Grasslands of Prairie Type — Wet Prairies on seasonally flooded lowlands. Dry Prairies on seldom flooded flatlands. Many former areas of this type are now improved pastures.

Hardwood Forests — Mixed evergreen and deciduous hardwoods, mostly on rich soil uplands.

Fresh Water Marshes — Some are mixed marshes of many kinds of herbs and bushes and some are dominated by one plant, such as the Saw Grass Marshes.

Wet to Dry Prairie-Marshes on Marl and Rockland — Some are mostly thin saw grass, others are bushes and grasses.

Swamp Forests, Mostly of Hardwoods — Several kinds bordering most rivers and in basins.

Sand Pine *(Pinus clausa)* **Scrub Forests** — Mostly on excessively drained, deep, sandy soils. These occur on old dunes along the coast and on old dunes or dry sands in the interior.

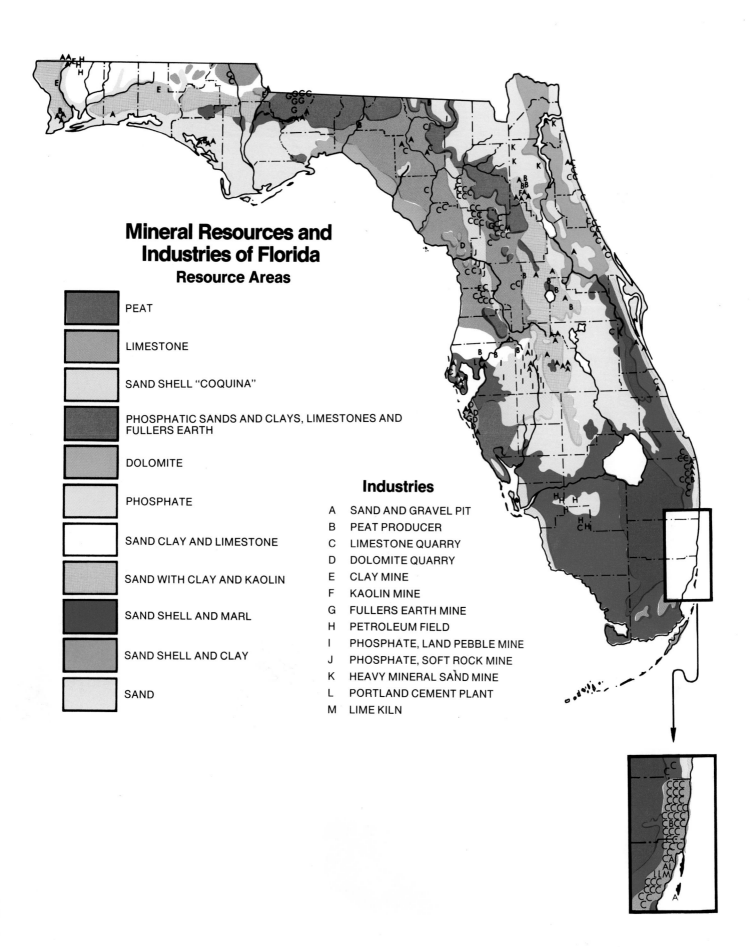

Mineral Resources and Industries of Florida
Resource Areas

- PEAT
- LIMESTONE
- SAND SHELL "COQUINA"
- PHOSPHATIC SANDS AND CLAYS, LIMESTONES AND FULLERS EARTH
- DOLOMITE
- PHOSPHATE
- SAND CLAY AND LIMESTONE
- SAND WITH CLAY AND KAOLIN
- SAND SHELL AND MARL
- SAND SHELL AND CLAY
- SAND

Industries

A   SAND AND GRAVEL PIT
B   PEAT PRODUCER
C   LIMESTONE QUARRY
D   DOLOMITE QUARRY
E   CLAY MINE
F   KAOLIN MINE
G   FULLERS EARTH MINE
H   PETROLEUM FIELD
I   PHOSPHATE, LAND PEBBLE MINE
J   PHOSPHATE, SOFT ROCK MINE
K   HEAVY MINERAL SAND MINE
L   PORTLAND CEMENT PLANT
M   LIME KILN

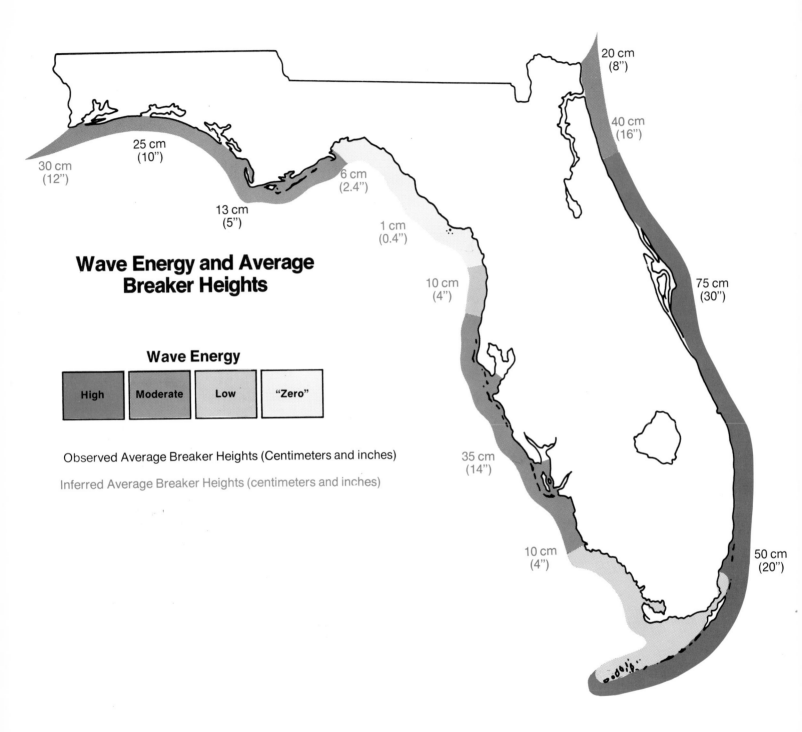

20 cm
(8")

40 cm
(16")

30 cm
(12")

25 cm
(10")

6 cm
(2.4")

13 cm
(5")

1 cm
(0.4")

75 cm
(30")

Wave Energy and Average Breaker Heights

10 cm
(4")

Wave Energy

High	Moderate	Low	"Zero"

Observed Average Breaker Heights (Centimeters and inches)

Inferred Average Breaker Heights (centimeters and inches)

35 cm
(14")

10 cm
(4")

50 cm
(20")

Water

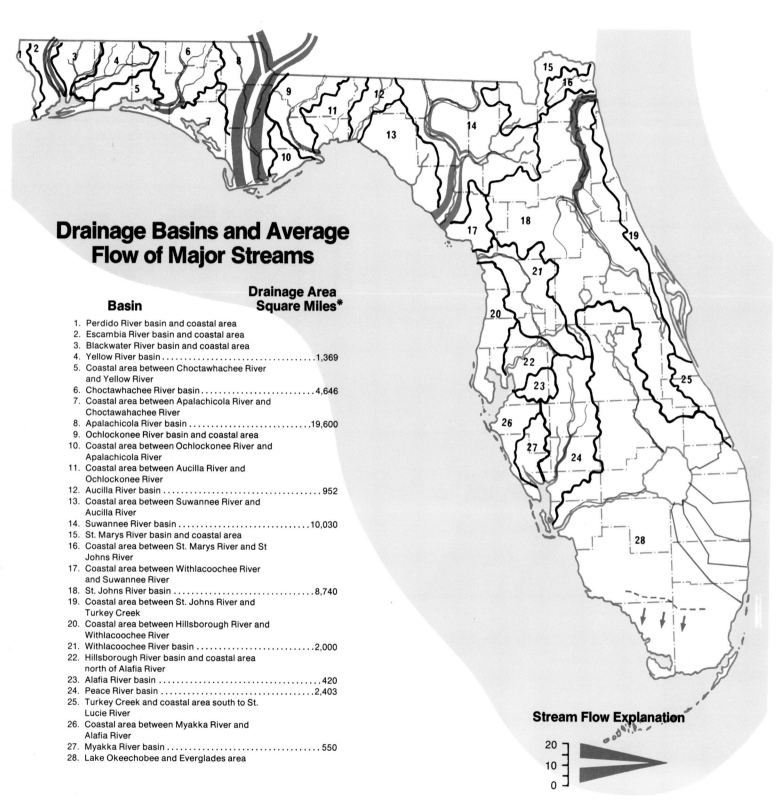

Drainage Basins and Average Flow of Major Streams

Basin	Drainage Area Square Miles*
1. Perdido River basin and coastal area	
2. Escambia River basin and coastal area	
3. Blackwater River basin and coastal area	
4. Yellow River basin	1,369
5. Coastal area between Choctawhachee River and Yellow River	
6. Choctawhachee River basin	4,646
7. Coastal area between Apalachicola River and Choctawahachee River	
8. Apalachicola River basin	19,600
9. Ochlockonee River basin and coastal area	
10. Coastal area between Ochlockonee River and Apalachicola River	
11. Coastal area between Aucilla River and Ochlockonee River	
12. Aucilla River basin	952
13. Coastal area between Suwannee River and Aucilla River	
14. Suwannee River basin	10,030
15. St. Marys River basin and coastal area	
16. Coastal area between St. Marys River and St Johns River	
17. Coastal area between Withlacoochee River and Suwannee River	
18. St. Johns River basin	8,740
19. Coastal area between St. Johns River and Turkey Creek	
20. Coastal area between Hillsborough River and Withlacoochee River	
21. Withlacoochee River basin	2,000
22. Hillsborough River basin and coastal area north of Alafia River	
23. Alafia River basin	420
24. Peace River basin	2,403
25. Turkey Creek and coastal area south to St. Lucie River	
26. Coastal area between Myakka River and Alafia River	
27. Myakka River basin	550
28. Lake Okeechobee and Everglades area	

*Drainage area values pertain only to individual drainage basins.

Stream Flow Explanation

Width of blue ribbon shows average flow of stream. Width of white ribbon shows flow during the month of lowest flow of record for the five largest streams. Scale values are in thousands of million gallons per day.

Seasonal Variation of Streamflow in Florida

Florida's pattern of streamflow variation is unusual in two respects. First, the month-to-month variation in average streamflow is relatively small; second, the seasonal variations of streams in different sections of the state are different. The small month-to-month variability in streamflow is the result of (1) relatively low variability of average monthly rainfall; (2) the relatively high rate of evapo-transpiration during the summer; (3) the large volume of slowly released natural storage in Florida's lakes; and (4) the large and relatively stable inflow of ground water to streams from extensive aquifer systems. Florida's unusual pattern of seasonal variation of streamflow is due predominantly to its position in the transition zone between the continental weather pattern of the southeastern United States and the tropical weather pattern of the Caribbean Sea. The continental pattern dominates in Northwestern Florida, a less continental and more tropical pattern in central Florida, and a largely tropical pattern in southern Florida.

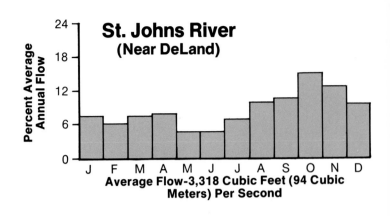

St. Johns River (Near DeLand)
Average Flow-3,318 Cubic Feet (94 Cubic Meters) Per Second

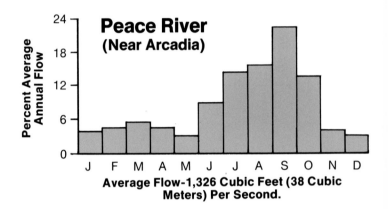

Peace River (Near Arcadia)
Average Flow-1,326 Cubic Feet (38 Cubic Meters) Per Second.

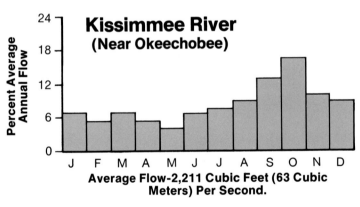

Kissimmee River (Near Okeechobee)
Average Flow-2,211 Cubic Feet (63 Cubic Meters) Per Second.

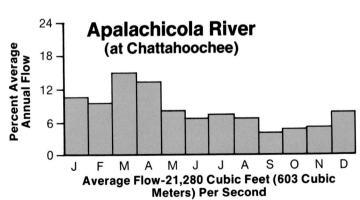

Apalachicola River (at Chattahoochee)
Average Flow-21,280 Cubic Feet (603 Cubic Meters) Per Second

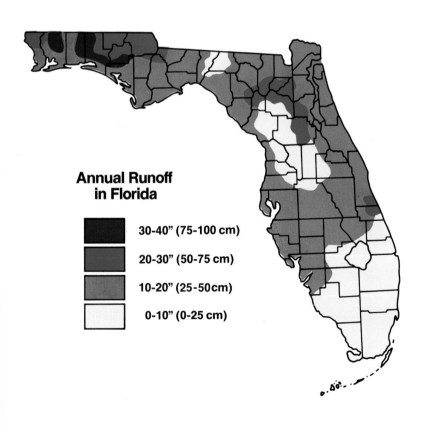

Annual Runoff in Florida

- 30-40" (75-100 cm)
- 20-30" (50-75 cm)
- 10-20" (25-50 cm)
- 0-10" (0-25 cm)

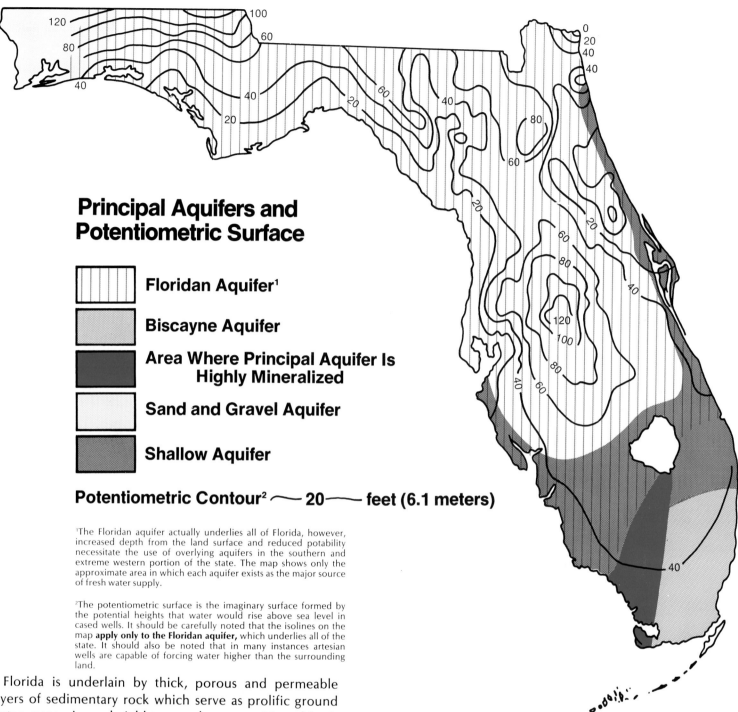

Principal Aquifers and Potentiometric Surface

	Floridan Aquifer[1]
	Biscayne Aquifer
	Area Where Principal Aquifer Is Highly Mineralized
	Sand and Gravel Aquifer
	Shallow Aquifer

Potentiometric Contour[2] — 20 — feet (6.1 meters)

[1]The Floridan aquifer actually underlies all of Florida, however, increased depth from the land surface and reduced potability necessitate the use of overlying aquifers in the southern and extreme western portion of the state. The map shows only the approximate area in which each aquifer exists as the major source of fresh water supply.

[2]The potentiometric surface is the imaginary surface formed by the potential heights that water would rise above sea level in cased wells. It should be carefully noted that the isolines on the map **apply only to the Floridan aquifer,** which underlies all of the state. It should also be noted that in many instances artesian wells are capable of forcing water higher than the surrounding land.

Florida is underlain by thick, porous and permeable layers of sedimentary rock which serve as prolific ground water reservoirs and yield tremendous quantities of fresh water to wells and some of the world's largest springs. These underground reservoirs are termed **aquifers** and are of two main types depending on the geologic formation that contains them. One type is the nonartesian or unconfined aquifer which is not blanketed above by an impervious rock layer. Its upper surface is referred to as the water table and withdrawal requires either pumping or direct use of exposed surface water. The second type is the artesian aquifer which is confined above by a less porous formation, and is under sufficient hydrostatic pressure to cause the water to rise over the containing layer where outlets such as springs or wells occur. The nature of the artesian aquifer makes pumping partially or completely

unnecessary for withdrawal.

The two major aquifers of Florida are the Floridan aquifer and the Biscayne aquifer. The Floridan is artesian in type and is the predominant source of fresh water for the state. Its water-yielding limestone layers average several hundred feet in thickness and lie close to the surface in the northern limits while descending to more than 1,000 feet below sea level in the southern portion. The Biscayne aquifer is nonartesian, as are the other aquifers shown on the map, and is wedge-shaped. It attains a maximum thickness of 100 to 400 feet along the eastern edge, but is reduced to only a few feet near its western limit.

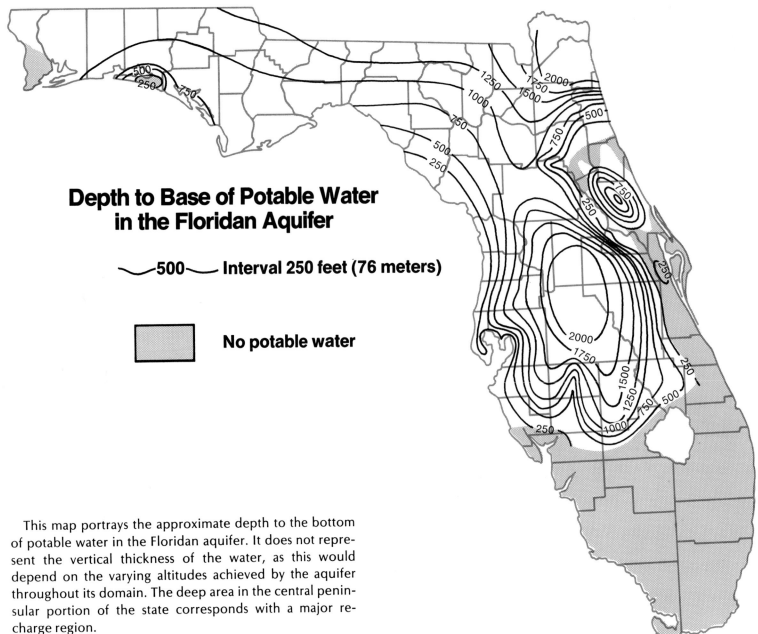

Depth to Base of Potable Water in the Floridan Aquifer

⌣500⌣ Interval 250 feet (76 meters)

▨ No potable water

This map portrays the approximate depth to the bottom of potable water in the Floridan aquifer. It does not represent the vertical thickness of the water, as this would depend on the varying altitudes achieved by the aquifer throughout its domain. The deep area in the central peninsular portion of the state corresponds with a major recharge region.

In this map, water is considered potable if its chloride content does not exceed 250 parts per million and its dissolved solids content does not exceed 500 parts per million. It should be noted that in areas marked as "no potable water", the fresh water supply source is, in most instances, from existing aquifers that overlie the Floridan aquifer and should not be interpreted as land areas void of potable water.

Major Florida Springs

Florida has 19 of the 75 first magnitude springs in the United States whose flow averages 100 cubic feet (2.8 cubic meters) per second or more.

The term *"hardness"* is applied to the soap neutralizing power of water. Soap will neither cleanse nor lather until all of the hardness is precipitated.

Hardness of ground water is caused by dissolved salts from the geologic formations through which the water has passed. Calcium and magnesium are usually the predominant hardness causing agents as others are seldom present in significant amounts.

Hardness is usually reported in terms of equivalent concentrations of calcium carbonate which is the amount of calcium carbonate required to cause a hardness equal to that caused by all the substances producing the hardness in water.

Although hard water has no reported harmful effects upon the health of the consumer, it does have detrimental qualities. These include excessive soap consumption, formation of scums and curds in homes, laundries and textile mills, yellowing of fabrics, toughening of vegetables cooked in hard water, and the formation of scale in boilers, hot water heaters, pipes and cooking utensils.

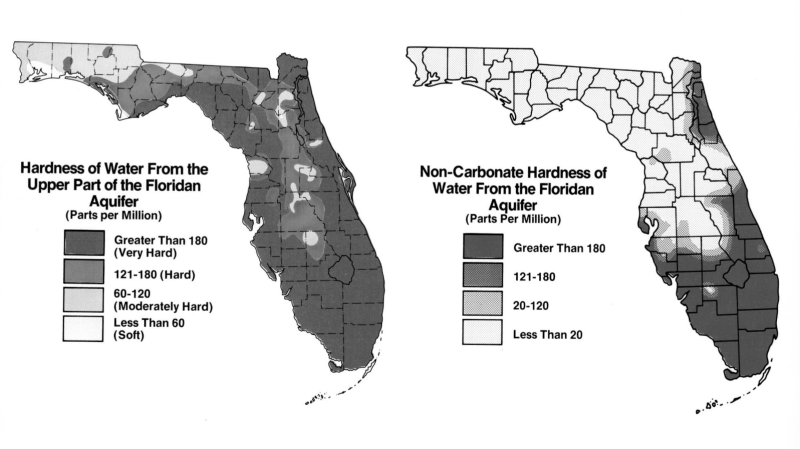

Hardness of Water From the Upper Part of the Floridan Aquifer
(Parts per Million)

- Greater Than 180 (Very Hard)
- 121-180 (Hard)
- 60-120 (Moderately Hard)
- Less Than 60 (Soft)

Non-Carbonate Hardness of Water From the Floridan Aquifer
(Parts Per Million)

- Greater Than 180
- 121-180
- 20-120
- Less Than 20

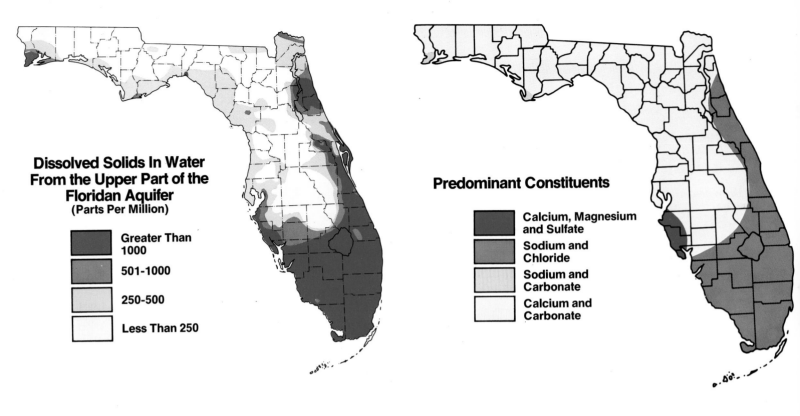

Dissolved Solids In Water From the Upper Part of the Floridan Aquifer
(Parts Per Million)

Greater Than 1000
501-1000
250-500
Less Than 250

Predominant Constituents

Calcium, Magnesium and Sulfate
Sodium and Chloride
Sodium and Carbonate
Calcium and Carbonate

Dissolved solids are a component of all natural water. A small percentage may be yielded through the solution of atmospheric impurities by rain, or by surface water contact with soluble materials. The major proportion of solids, however, is introduced through ground water percolating downward dissolving rocks and minerals or mixing with highly mineralized connate water (water that was trapped in the rocks at the time they were formed) , intruding seawater from the ocean, or pollution.

The four predominant constituent solids of the Floridan aquifer, which underlies all of Florida, are shown on the above map. The solution of limestone deposits accounts for the large area of calcium and carbonate. The sodium and chloride concentration results from the encroachment of salt water into the aquifer or through mixing with connate water.

The amount of dissolved solids is an important consideration when determining water quality for human consumption and industrial use. The United States Public Health Service recommends that dissolved solid content of drinking water not exceed 500 parts per million if other, less mineralized, water is available. Water containing solids in excess of 2,000 parts per million may not quench thirst and may have a laxative effect on the user; however, no permanent, harmful effects have been reported. Dissolved solids in industrial waters can cause foaming in boilers and interference with clarity, color, or taste of many finished products.

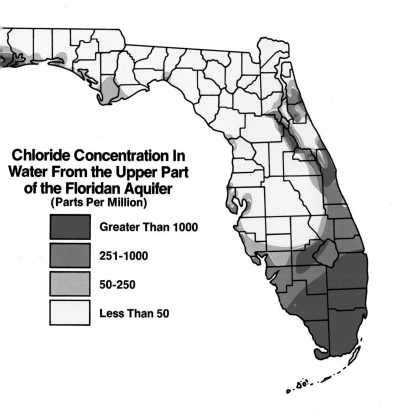

Chloride Concentration In Water From the Upper Part of the Floridan Aquifer
(Parts Per Million)

- Greater Than 1000
- 251-1000
- 50-250
- Less Than 50

This map shows the approximate pattern of chloride concentration of water in the upper part of the Floridan aquifer. Below this part, water high in chloride content can be found everywhere in the state. In areas where water from the Floridan aquifer has a chloride concentration that does not meet water quality standards, fresh, usable water is usually available in overlying, shallow aquifers.

Chloride occurs in almost all natural water. Some chloride is contained in rainwater and some is dissolved from land surface materials. The amount of chloride contributed from these sources is generally small in Florida. After the water enters the ground, however, the concentration normally increases. This increase may result from the solution of rocks and minerals, mixing with connate water (water that was trapped in the rocks at the time they were formed), encroachment of salt water from the ocean, or pollution.

The United States Public Health Service recommends that chloride in drinking water not exceed 250 parts per million. This is based on palatability rather than health requirements.

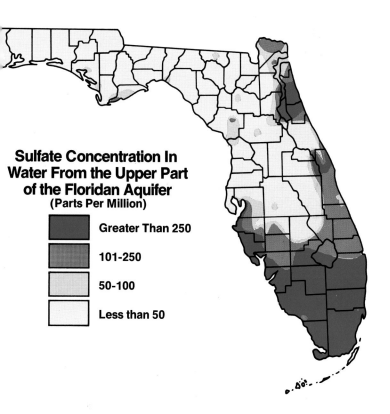

Sulfate Concentration In Water From the Upper Part of the Floridan Aquifer
(Parts Per Million)

- Greater Than 250
- 101-250
- 50-100
- Less than 50

In the Floridan aquifer, which underlies all of Florida, sulfate concentration tends to be higher in the deeper zones. This map portrays only the upper portion of the aquifer.

Sulfate occurs in almost all natural water. It may be dissolved in rainwater from atmospheric gases and impurities or in surface water from materials on the ground.

The amount of sulfate yielded by these sources is normally small. Sulfate may also be discharged in numerous industrial wastes.

After the water enters the ground, the sulfate concentration generally increases. This increase may result from the leaching of gypsum and other sulfate minerals as the water percolates through the ground. Other sources include connate water (water that was trapped in the rocks at the time they were formed), salt water from the ocean, or pollutants.

The United States Public Health Service recommends that sulfates not exceed 250 parts per million in drinking water when a more suitable supply is available. Public water supplies with a sulfate concentration above 250 parts per million are commonly used without adverse effect other than in taste and a possible laxative action on the new user.

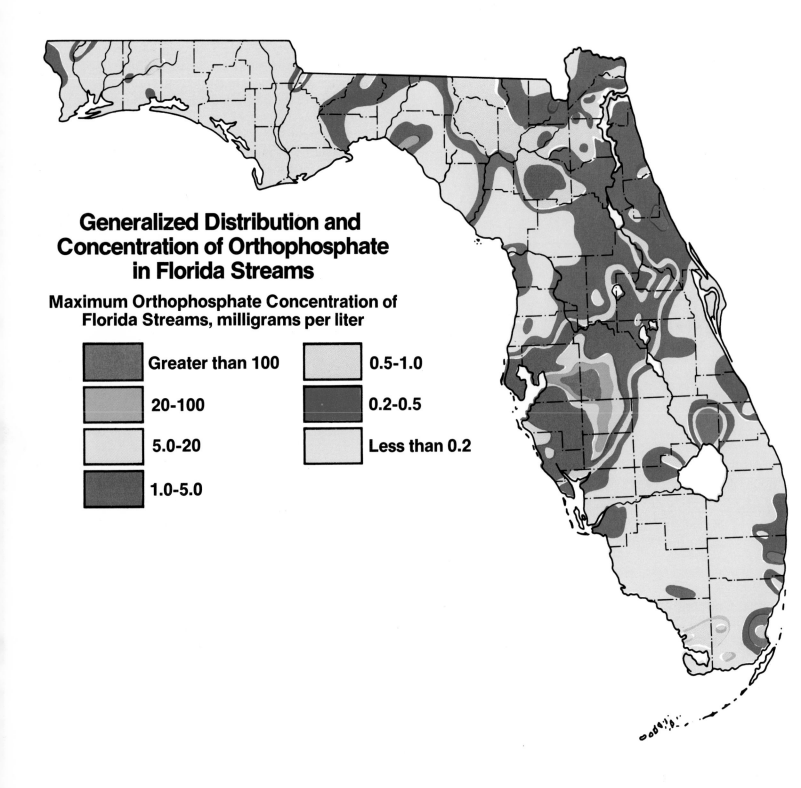

Generalized Distribution and Concentration of Orthophosphate in Florida Streams

Maximum Orthophosphate Concentration of Florida Streams, milligrams per liter

Greater than 100

20-100

5.0-20

1.0-5.0

0.5-1.0

0.2-0.5

Less than 0.2

A growing realization that fresh water is a critical resource has placed an increased emphasis on more accurate methods of monitoring its withdrawal and use. This trend became particularly apparent during the late 60's so that it is likely that data for 1970 water withdrawal was more accurately compiled than the data for 1965. Referring to the "Florida's Fresh Water" graph, irrigation in Florida during 1965 was probably overestimated. This is indicated by its drastic deviation from the graphic trend established by the other years of measurement.

In comparing the relative measurement reliability and accuracy of one type of water withdrawal data to another, *Irrigation* is subject to the greatest amount of error. Conveyance losses and other hard-to-measure variables make it difficult to obtain accurate and consistent estimates of withdrawal. However, *Public Supply* can be measured with relative precision because it is almost entirely a metered supply.

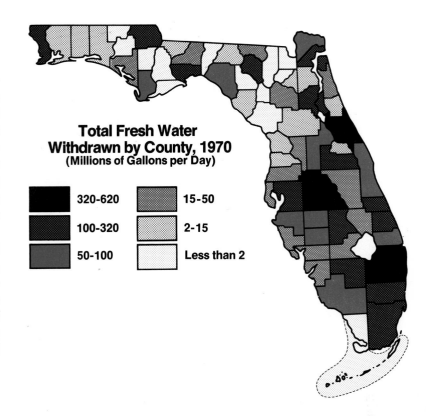

Total Fresh Water Withdrawn by County, 1970
(Millions of Gallons per Day)

320-620	15-50
100-320	2-15
50-100	Less than 2

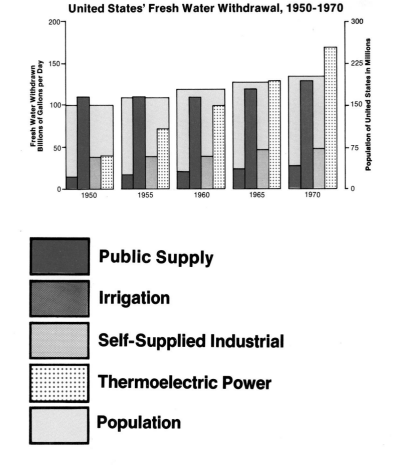

United States' Fresh Water Withdrawal, 1950-1970

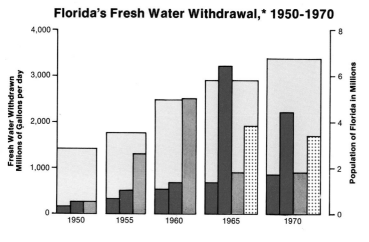

Florida's Fresh Water Withdrawal,* 1950-1970

Public Supply

Irrigation

Self-Supplied Industrial

Thermoelectric Power

Population

*Withdrawal data for *Self-supplied Industrial* and *Thermoelectric Power* were combined for 1950, 1955 and 1960.

The decrease in thermoelectric power withdrawal from 1960 to 1970 reveals only a decrease in fresh water use. Increasingly, saline surface water is being used in coastal plants.

Fresh Water Use in Florida, 1970

These maps were adapted from unpublished material prepared by the United States Geological Survey in cooperation with the Bureau of Geology, Florida Department of Natural Resources.

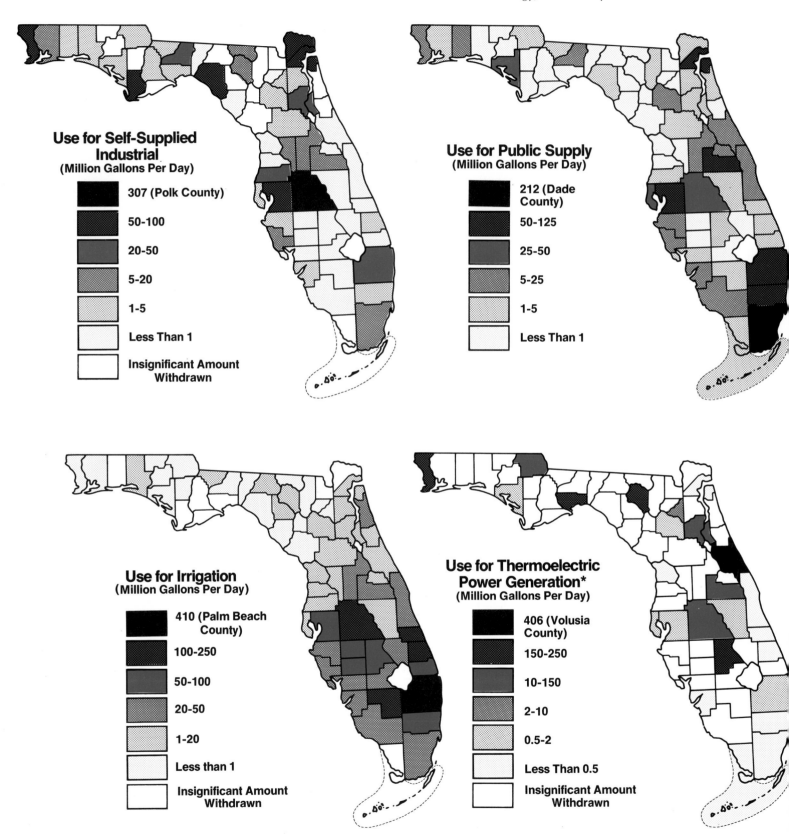

Use for Self-Supplied Industrial
(Million Gallons Per Day)

- 307 (Polk County)
- 50-100
- 20-50
- 5-20
- 1-5
- Less Than 1
- Insignificant Amount Withdrawn

Use for Public Supply
(Million Gallons Per Day)

- 212 (Dade County)
- 50-125
- 25-50
- 5-25
- 1-5
- Less Than 1

Use for Irrigation
(Million Gallons Per Day)

- 410 (Palm Beach County)
- 100-250
- 50-100
- 20-50
- 1-20
- Less than 1
- Insignificant Amount Withdrawn

Use for Thermoelectric Power Generation*
(Million Gallons Per Day)

- 406 (Volusia County)
- 150-250
- 10-150
- 2-10
- 0.5-2
- Less Than 0.5
- Insignificant Amount Withdrawn

*The values do not necessarily represent the intensity of thermo-electric power generation within the particular county, as many coastal plants use predominantly saline water rather than fresh.

Climate

Climate is probably Florida's greatest natural resource. General climatic conditions range from a zone of transition between temperate and subtropical conditions in the extreme northern interior portion of the state to the tropical conditions found on the Florida Keys. The chief factors of climatic control are: latitude, proximity to the Atlantic Ocean and Gulf of Mexico, and numerous inland lakes.

Summers throughout the state are long, warm, and relatively humid; winter, although punctuated with periodic invasions of cool to occasionally cold air from the north, are mild because of the southern latitude and relatively warm adjacent ocean waters. The Gulf Stream, which flows around the western tip of Cuba through the Straits of Florida and northward along the lower east coast, exerts a warming influence to the southern east coast largely because the predominant wind direction is from the east. Coastal stations throughout the state average slightly warmer in winter and cooler in summer than do inland stations at the same latitude.

Florida enjoys abundant rainfall. Except for the northwestern portion of the state, the average year can be divided into two seasons — the so-called "rainy season" and the long, relatively dry season. On the peninsula, generally more than one-half of the precipitation for an average year can be expected to fall during the 4-month period, June through September. In northwest Florida, there is a secondary rainfall maximum in late winter and early spring.

Mean annual temperatures range from the upper 60's in the northern portions of the state to the middle 70's on the southern mainland, but reach nearly 78° at Key West. Summertime mean temperatures are about the same throughout the state, 81° to 82°; during the coolest months, temperatures average about 13° lower in northern than in southern Florida. July and August temperature averages are the warmest in all areas, and December and January temperature averages are the coolest in the northern and central portions of the state. January and February, on the average, are the coolest months in the extreme south and on the Keys.

Maximum temperatures during the warmest months average near 90° along the coast and slightly above 90° in the interior; minima average is in the low 70's inland but are slightly higher along the immediate coast and on the Keys. During June, July, and August, maximum temperatures exceed 90° about 2 days in 3 in all interior areas. In May and September, 90° or higher can be expected about 1 day in 3 in the northern interior and about 1 day in 2 in the southern interior. Extreme heat waves, characteristic of continental locations, are felt occasionally—but in a modified form—over the northern interior portions of Florida. Temperatures of 100° or higher are infrequent in northern, rare in central, and practically unknown in

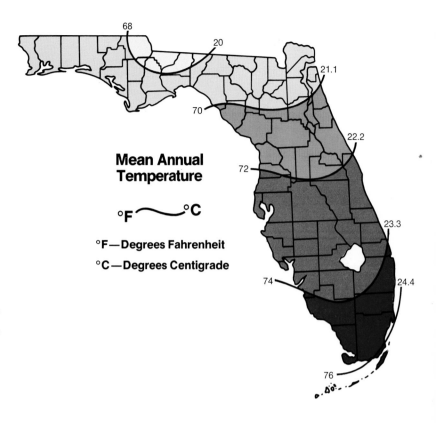

Mean Annual Temperature

°F ~ °C

°F—Degrees Fahrenheit
°C—Degrees Centigrade

southern Florida.

The summer heat is tempered by sea breezes along the coast and by frequent afternoon or early evening thunderstorms in all areas. Gentle breezes occur almost daily in all areas and serve to mitigate further the oppressiveness that otherwise would accompany the prevailing summer temperature and humidity conditions. Because most of the large-scale wind patterns affecting Florida have passed over water surfaces, hot drying winds seldom occur.

Although average minimum temperatures during the coolest months range from the middle 40's in the north to the middle 50's in the south, no place on the mainland is entirely safe from frost or freezing. An occasional cold wave of the more severe type brings minima, ranging from 50° to 20° over the northern portions to freezing or below over the southern portions of the peninsula. These cold waves, except in rare instances, seldom last more than 2 or 3 days at a time. It is extremely rare for temperatures to remain below freezing throughout the day at any place in the state.

Extreme Highest and Lowest Recorded Temperatures*
Degrees Fahrenheit

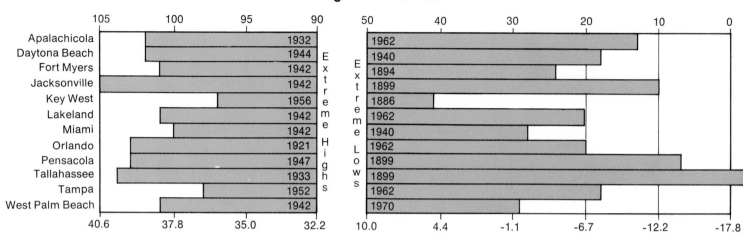

	Extreme Highs	Extreme Lows
Apalachicola	1932	1962
Daytona Beach	1944	1940
Fort Myers	1942	1894
Jacksonville	1942	1899
Key West	1956	1886
Lakeland	1942	1962
Miami	1942	1940
Orlando	1921	1962
Pensacola	1947	1899
Tallahassee	1933	1899
Tampa	1952	1962
West Palm Beach	1942	1970

Degrees Centigrade

*The reader should note that the period of weather observation (number of years over which the data was accumulated) may differ from one station to the next, thus caution should be used when comparing localities.

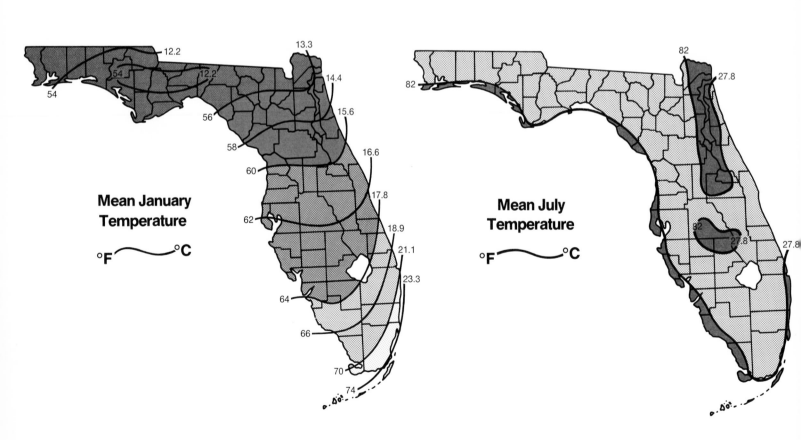

Mean January Temperature °F ⌒ °C

Mean July Temperature °F ⌒ °C

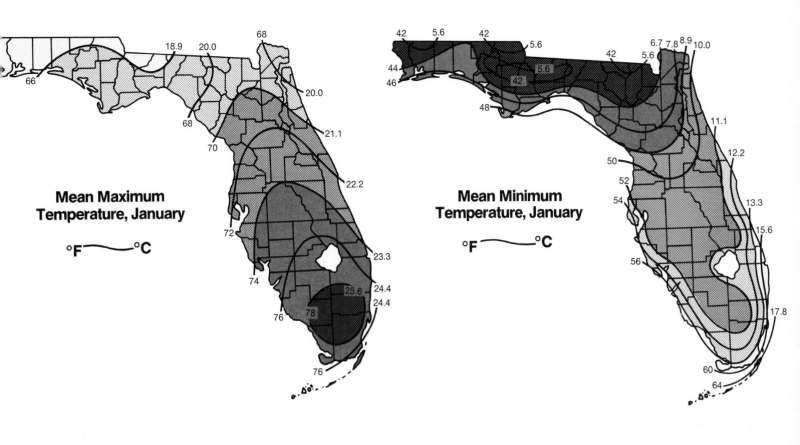

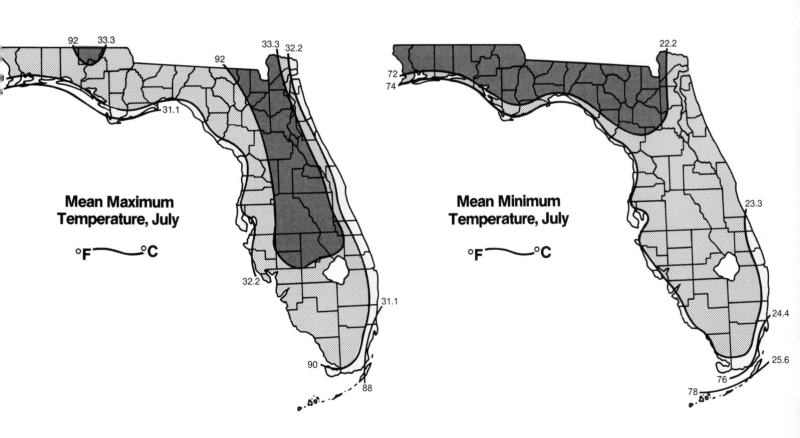

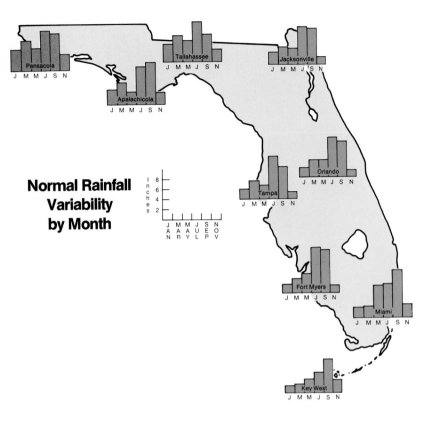

Normal Rainfall Variability by Month

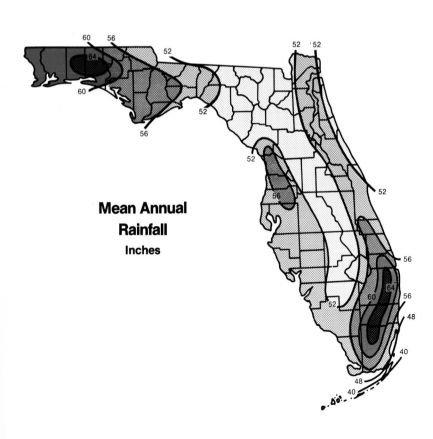

Mean Annual Rainfall

Inches

PRECIPITATION. Rainfall in Florida is quite varied both in annual amount and in seasonal distribution. Individual station annual averages, based upon the 30-year period, 1931-1960, range from about 50 to 65 inches. On the Keys, annual averages are only about 40 inches. High annual rainfall is measured at stations in the extreme northwestern counties and in the southern end of the peninsula. Rainfall varies greatly from year to year, with wet years sometimes doubling the amounts received during a dry year. Many localities have received more than 80 inches in a calendar year, and a few stations have measured more than 100 inches. In contrast, almost all localities have received less than 40 inches in a calendar year.

The distribution of rainfall within the year is quite uneven. In the summer rainy season, there is close to a 50-50 chance that some rain will fall on any given day. During the remainder of the year, the chances of rainfall are much less, with some rain being likely to fall on 1 or 2 days in a week.

The seasonal distribution changes somewhat from north to south. In the northwestern portions of the state, there are two high points — late winter or early spring and again during summer — and one pronounced low point — October; a secondary low point occurs in April and May. On the peninsula, the most striking features of the seasonal distribution are the dominance of summer rainfall (generally more than one-half of the average annual amount falls in the 4-month period, June through September) and the rather abrupt start and end of the summer rainy season. (June average rainfall tends to be nearly double the amount of May and in the fall, the average for the last month of the wet season tends to be about double the amount of the following month). October averages as the driest month in northwest Florida, but, in general, is among the wettest months on the southeast coast and Keys.

The start and end of the rainy season varies considerably from year to year. According to climatic records, the season has begun as soon as early May and has been as delayed as late June. Late September or early October usually marks the end of the wet season, except along a narrow strip of the entire east coast where relatively large October rainfalls are frequently noted. The tendency for relatively large October rainfall diminishes quite rapidly westward.

Most of the summer rainfall is derived from "local" showers or thundershowers. Many stations average more than 80 thundershowers per year, and some average more than 100. Showers are often heavy, usually lasting only 1 or 2 hours, and generally occur near the hottest part of the day. The more severe thundershowers are occasionally attended by hail or locally strong winds which may inflict serious local damage to crops and property. Day-long summer rains are usually associated with tropical disturbances and are infrequent. Even in the wet season, the rainfall duration is generally less than 10 percent of the time.

Because most summer rains are local in character, large differences in monthly and annual amounts at nearby stations are common, but these differences disappear when a comparison is made on the basis of long-period averages. However, large differences in the long-period averages do exist within short distances. For example, the normal annual rainfalls for Miami Beach and for the Miami Airport are 46.26 and 59.76 inches, respectively, yet it is less than 10 airline miles distance from the Beach to the Airport. Similar conditions undoubtedly exist elsewhere along the immediate coast.

Most localities have, at one time or another, experienced 2-hour rainfalls in excess of 3 inches and 24-hour amounts of near or greater than 10 inches. Nearly all localities have had within a single month from one-third to one-half as much rain as will fall during an entire average year. Occasionally, tropical storms produce copious rainfall over relatively large areas. A detailed survey of the September 1950 hurricane, conducted by the U. S. Corps of Engineers Florida District, headquartered at Jacksonville, indicated an amount that was near 34 inches fell in a 24-hour period within the vicinity of Cedar Key. The 38.70 inches of rainfall that fell during the 24-hour period at Yankeetown on September 5-6, 1950, is the record 24-hour rainfall for the Nation. Because of water disposal problems, heavy rains can be just as serious as droughts.

DROUGHTS. Florida is not immune from drought, even though annual rainfall amounts are relatively large. Prolonged periods of deficient rainfall are occasionally experienced even during the time of the expected rainy season. Several such dry periods, in the course of 1 or 2 years, can lead to significantly lowered water tables and lake levels which, in turn, may cause serious water shortages for those communities that depend upon lakes and shallow wells for their water supply. The worst drought in over 40 years along the Lower East Coast Division occurred in 1971. In that Division, the lowest 12-month rainfall of record, 34.59 inches, was set during the period from July 1970 to June 1971. The level of Lake Okeechobee dropped to 10.3 feet, only 0.16 of a foot above the record minimum of 10.14 feet.

Because a large part of the state's agricultural produce is planted, grown, and marketed during fall, winter, and spring (normally the driest part of the year), growers of high-per-acre-value crops have long concluded that it is almost mandatory to provide supplemental irrigation for crop success. The flat topography of the area where many of these crops are grown is well suited to subsurface irrigation by water table control. However, heavy rains can occur during these growing seasons, and growers have found it necessary to provide water-removal facilities in addition to those for irrigation.

Statewide droughts during summer are rare, but it is not unusual during a drought in one portion of the state for other portions to receive generous rainfall. In a few instances, individual stations have experienced periods of a month or more without rainfall.

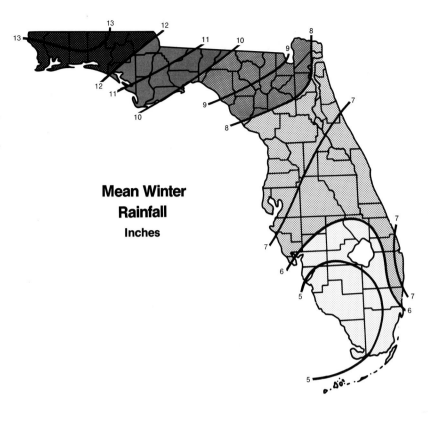

Mean Winter Rainfall
Inches

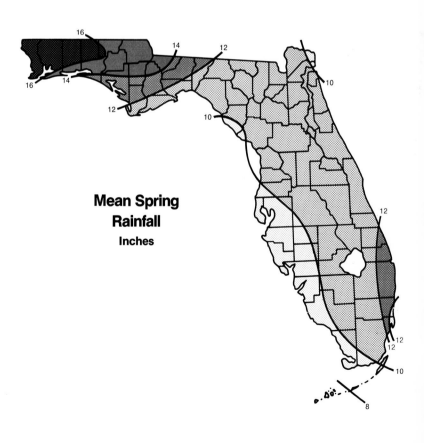

Mean Spring Rainfall
Inches

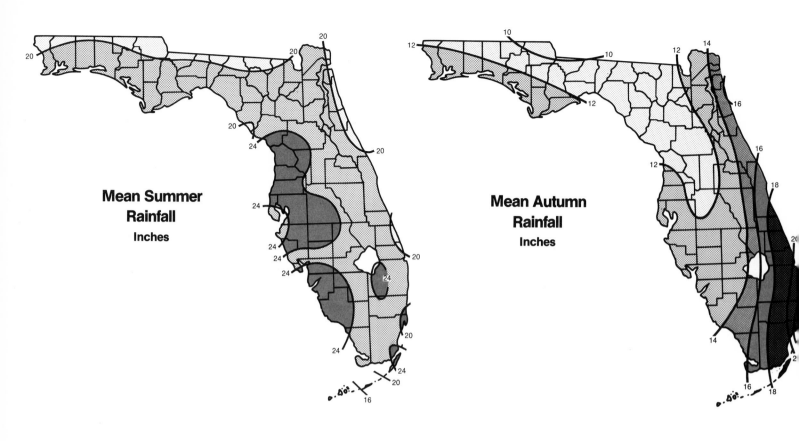

Mean Summer Rainfall
Inches

Mean Autumn Rainfall
Inches

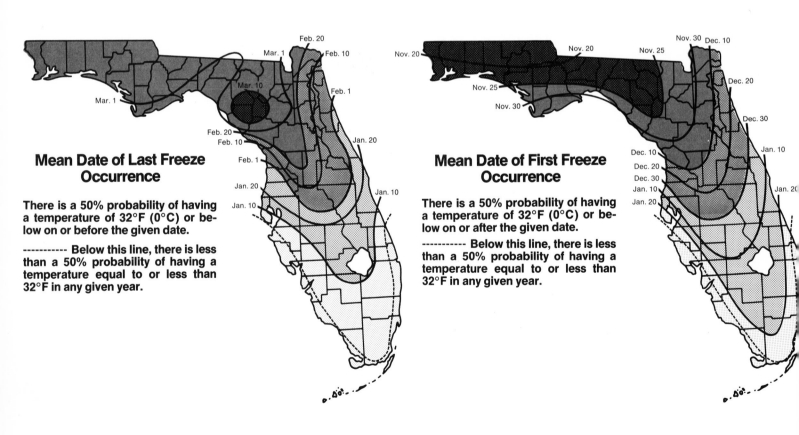

Mean Date of Last Freeze Occurrence

There is a 50% probability of having a temperature of 32°F (0°C) or below on or before the given date.

---------- Below this line, there is less than a 50% probability of having a temperature equal to or less than 32°F in any given year.

Mean Date of First Freeze Occurrence

There is a 50% probability of having a temperature of 32°F (0°C) or below on or after the given date.

---------- Below this line, there is less than a 50% probability of having a temperature equal to or less than 32°F in any given year.

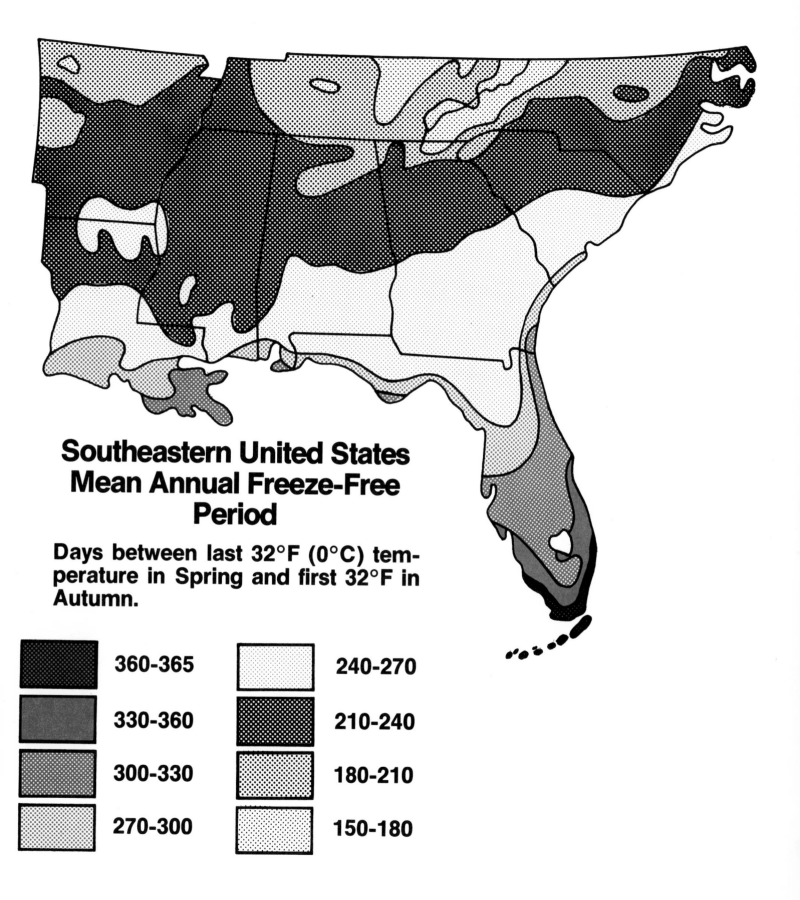

Southeastern United States Mean Annual Freeze-Free Period

Days between last 32°F (0°C) temperature in Spring and first 32°F in Autumn.

360-365	240-270
330-360	210-240
300-330	180-210
270-300	150-180

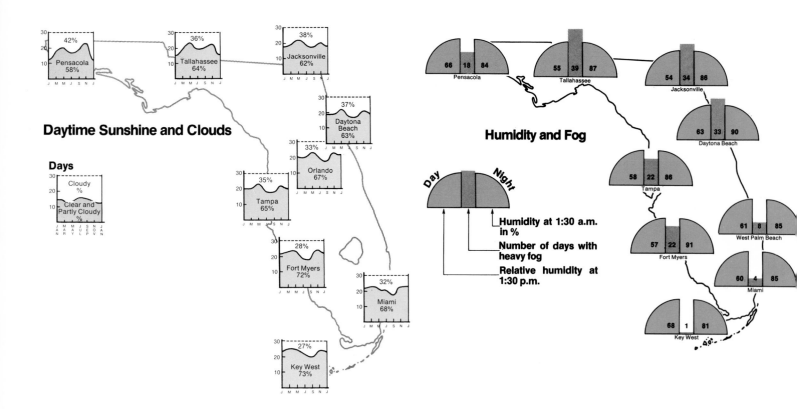

Daytime Sunshine and Clouds

Days

Cloudy %

Clear and Partly Cloudy %

Humidity and Fog

Day Night

Humidity at 1:30 a.m. in %

Number of days with heavy fog

Relative humidity at 1:30 p.m.

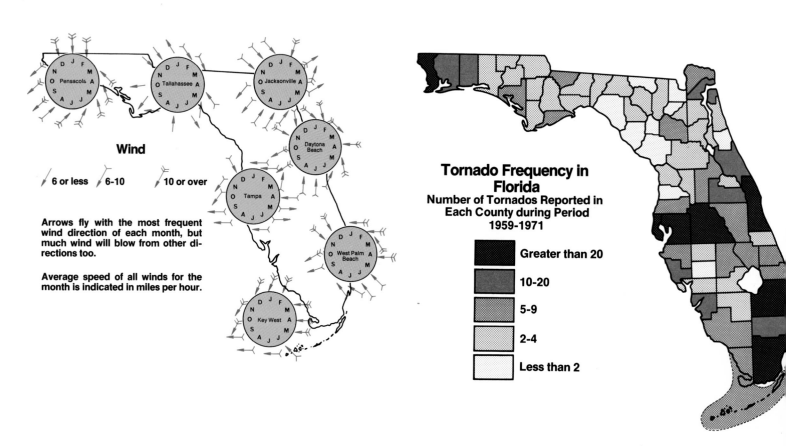

Wind

6 or less   6-10   10 or over

Arrows fly with the most frequent wind direction of each month, but much wind will blow from other directions too.

Average speed of all winds for the month is indicated in miles per hour.

Tornado Frequency in Florida
Number of Tornados Reported in Each County during Period 1959-1971

- Greater than 20
- 10-20
- 5-9
- 2-4
- Less than 2

Note that the most populous areas have reported the greater number of tornados. A tornado may occur in an unpopulated area and go unreported. In several cases, a storm may be counted twice when it affects more than one county.

Mean Frequency of Tornados by Months from 1959-1971

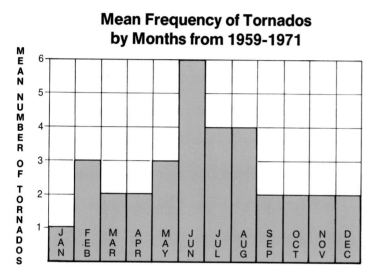

Frequency of Florida Hurricanes by Months from 1885 to 1965

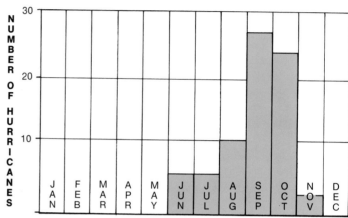

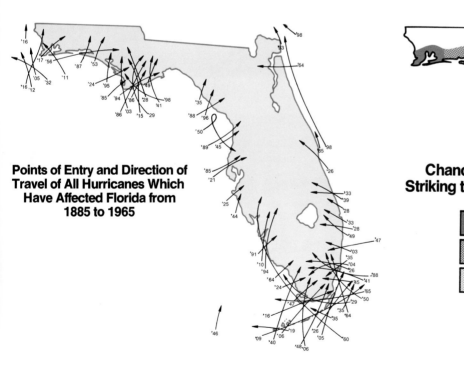

Points of Entry and Direction of Travel of All Hurricanes Which Have Affected Florida from 1885 to 1965

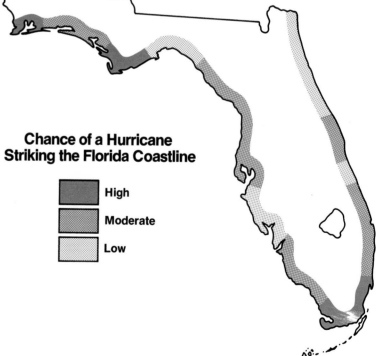

Chance of a Hurricane Striking the Florida Coastline

High
Moderate
Low

Transportation and Communication

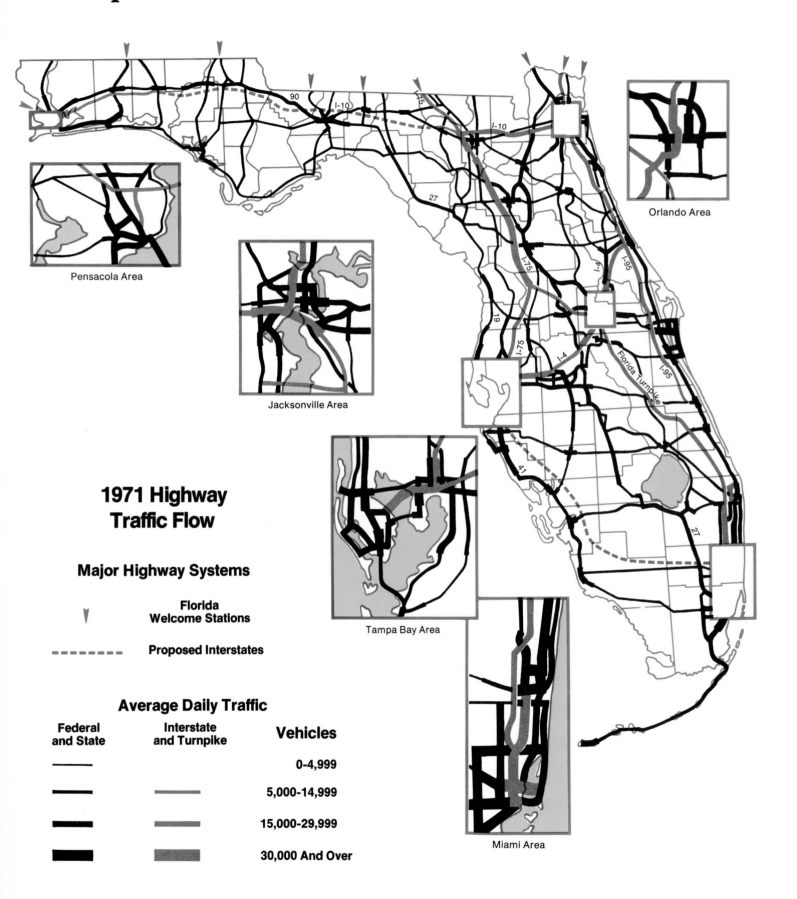

1971 Highway Traffic Flow

Major Highway Systems

∨ **Florida Welcome Stations**

- - - - - - - **Proposed Interstates**

Average Daily Traffic

Federal and State	Interstate and Turnpike	Vehicles
——		0-4,999
——	——	5,000-14,999
——	——	15,000-29,999
——	——	30,000 And Over

Pensacola Area

Jacksonville Area

Orlando Area

Tampa Bay Area

Miami Area

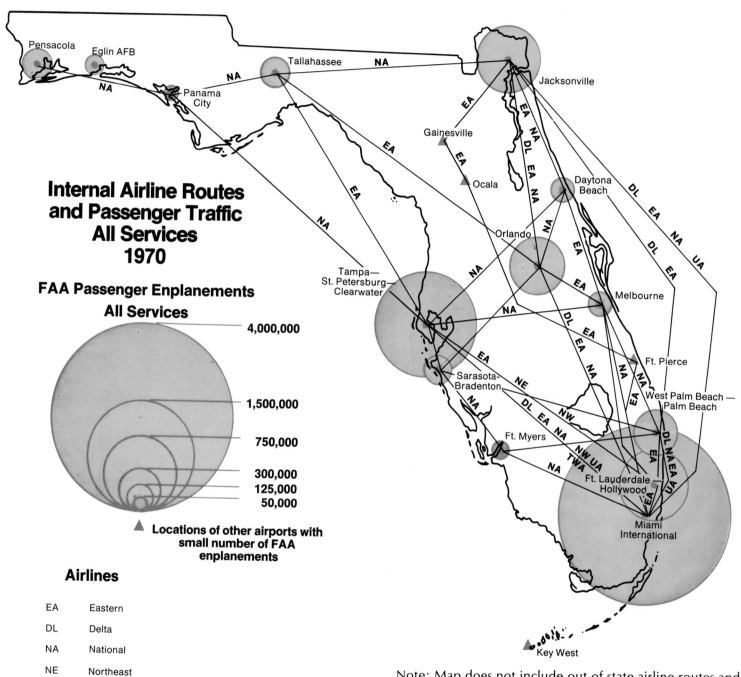

Internal Airline Routes and Passenger Traffic All Services 1970

FAA Passenger Enplanements
All Services

4,000,000

1,500,000

750,000

300,000
125,000
50,000

▲ Locations of other airports with small number of FAA enplanements

Airlines

EA	Eastern
DL	Delta
NA	National
NE	Northeast
NW	Northwest
TWA	TransWorld
UA	United

Note: Map does not include out of state airline routes and less important routes between Florida Airports. Eglin Air Force Base handles civilian air passenger traffic as well as military.

Railroads, 1970

————	SCL	Seaboard Coast Line
••••••••	FEC	Florida East Coast
————	L & N	Louisville & Nashville
– – – – –	GS & F	Georgia Southern & Florida
	LOP & G	Live Oak, Perry & Gulf
	SG	South Georgia
	VS	Valdosta Southern
••••••••	ST L & SF	St. Louis & San Francisco
	A & ST AB	Atlanta & St. Andrews Bay
	AN	Apalachicola Northern
	M & B	Marianna & Blountstown

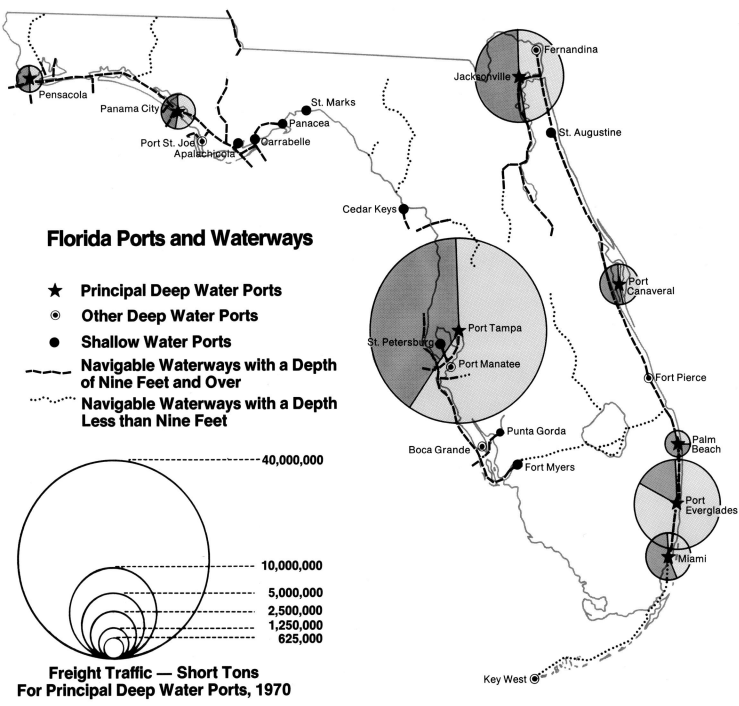

Florida Ports and Waterways

★ **Principal Deep Water Ports**

◉ **Other Deep Water Ports**

● **Shallow Water Ports**

– – – **Navigable Waterways with a Depth of Nine Feet and Over**

········· **Navigable Waterways with a Depth Less than Nine Feet**

40,000,000

10,000,000

5,000,000

2,500,000

1,250,000

625,000

Freight Traffic — Short Tons For Principal Deep Water Ports, 1970

Foreign | Domestic

Proportional Distribution of Foreign and Domestic Freight Volume

It should be noted that tonnage is only one index of a port's character and does not necessarily indicate value or intensity of shipping; e.g., Tampa's large volume of phosphate handled accounts for the representative symbol for tonnage being almost four times that of Miami or Jacksonville even though both of these ports have freight values three times that of Tampa's.

Florida has fourteen deep water commercial ports (depth 27 feet or more) and nine major shallow water ports (depth 8 to 27 feet) situated along its 1,300 miles of coastline. Florida ports have moderate tides, averaging less than 3 feet, and nearly all have very short, easily navigated approaches from and to open ocean waters.

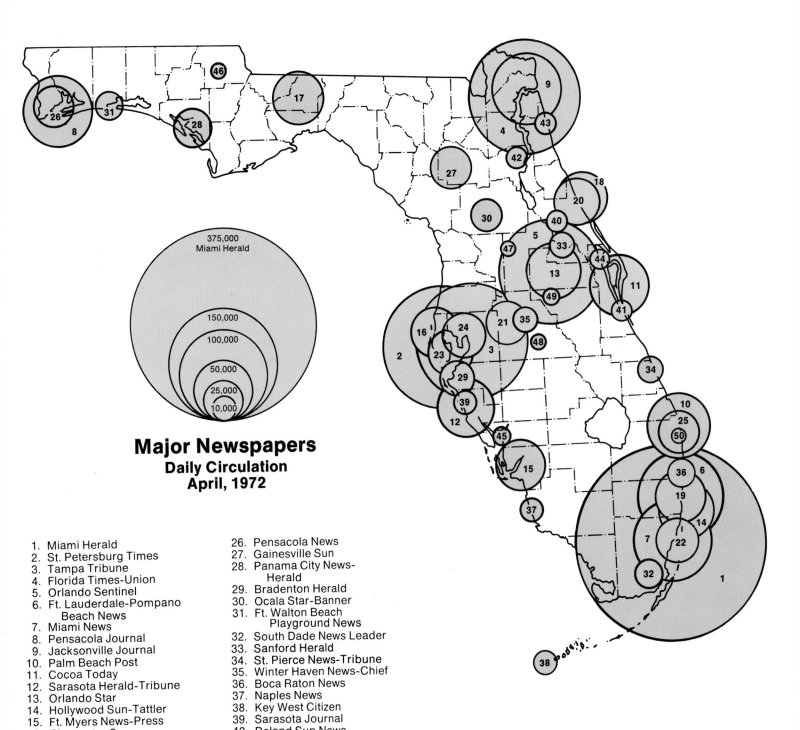

Major Newspapers
Daily Circulation
April, 1972

375,000
Miami Herald

150,000

100,000

50,000

25,000

10,000

1. Miami Herald
2. St. Petersburg Times
3. Tampa Tribune
4. Florida Times-Union
5. Orlando Sentinel
6. Ft. Lauderdale-Pompano
   Beach News
7. Miami News
8. Pensacola Journal
9. Jacksonville Journal
10. Palm Beach Post
11. Cocoa Today
12. Sarasota Herald-Tribune
13. Orlando Star
14. Hollywood Sun-Tattler
15. Ft. Myers News-Press
16. Clearwater Sun
17. Tallahassee Democrat
18. Daytona Beach Journal
19. Ft. Lauderdale-Pompano Beach
    Sun Sentinel
20. Daytona Beach News
21. Lakeland Ledger
22. Miami Beach Sun-Reporter
23. St. Petersburg Independent
24. Tampa Times
25. Palm Beach Times

26. Pensacola News
27. Gainesville Sun
28. Panama City News-
    Herald
29. Bradenton Herald
30. Ocala Star-Banner
31. Ft. Walton Beach
    Playground News
32. South Dade News Leader
33. Sanford Herald
34. St. Pierce News-Tribune
35. Winter Haven News-Chief
36. Boca Raton News
37. Naples News
38. Key West Citizen
39. Sarasota Journal
40. Deland Sun News
41. Melbourne Times
42. Palatka News
43. St. Augustine Record
44. Titusville Star-Advocate
45. Punta Gorda Herald-News
46. Jackson County Floridian
47. Leesburg Commercial
48. Lake Wales Highlander
49. Osceola Sun
50. Palm Beach News

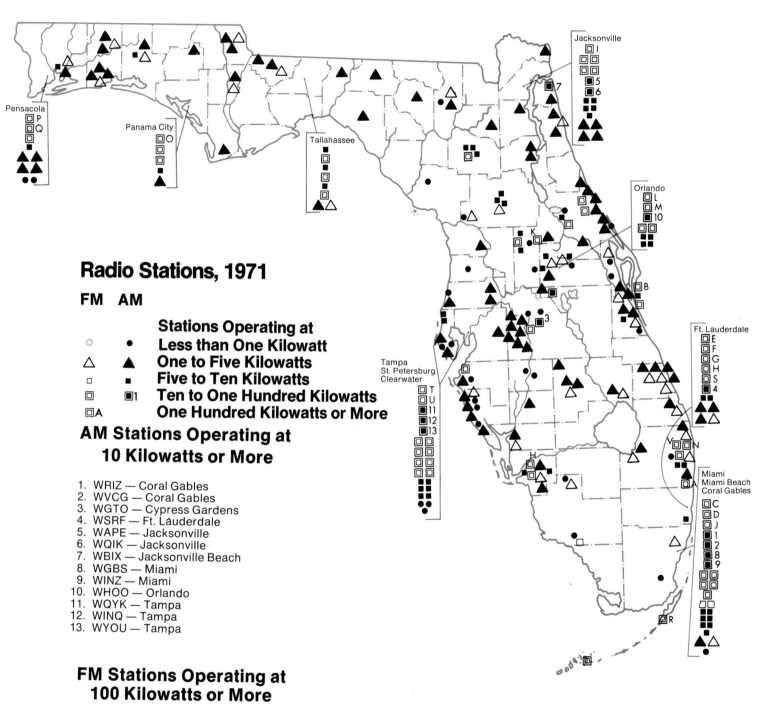

Radio Stations, 1971

FM   AM

		Stations Operating at
○	●	**Less than One Kilowatt**
△	▲	**One to Five Kilowatts**
□	■	**Five to Ten Kilowatts**
▣	▣1	**Ten to One Hundred Kilowatts**
▣A		**One Hundred Kilowatts or More**

AM Stations Operating at 10 Kilowatts or More

1. WRIZ — Coral Gables
2. WVCG — Coral Gables
3. WGTO — Cypress Gardens
4. WSRF — Ft. Lauderdale
5. WAPE — Jacksonville
6. WQIK — Jacksonville
7. WBIX — Jacksonville Beach
8. WGBS — Miami
9. WINZ — Miami
10. WHOO — Orlando
11. WQYK — Tampa
12. WINQ — Tampa
13. WYOU — Tampa

FM Stations Operating at 100 Kilowatts or More

A. WWOG — Boca Raton
B. WCKS — Cocoa Beach
C. WLYF — Coral Gables
D. WFOR — Coral Gables
E. WAXY — Ft. Lauderdale
F. WFTL-FM — Ft. Lauderdale
G. WSHE — Ft. Lauderdale
H. WMJR — Ft. Lauderdale
I. WPDQ — Jacksonville
J. WMYQ — Miami
K. WORJ-FM — Mt. Dora

L. WDIZ-FM — Orlando
M. WDBO-FM — Orlando
N. WMUM — Palm Beach
O. WGNE-FM — Panama City
P. WBOP-FM — Pensacola
Q. WPEX-FM — Pensacola
R. WXOS — Plantation Key
S. WCKO — Pompano Beach
T. WLCY-FM — St. Petersburg
U. WFLA-FM — Tampa
V. WEAT-FM — W. Palm Beach

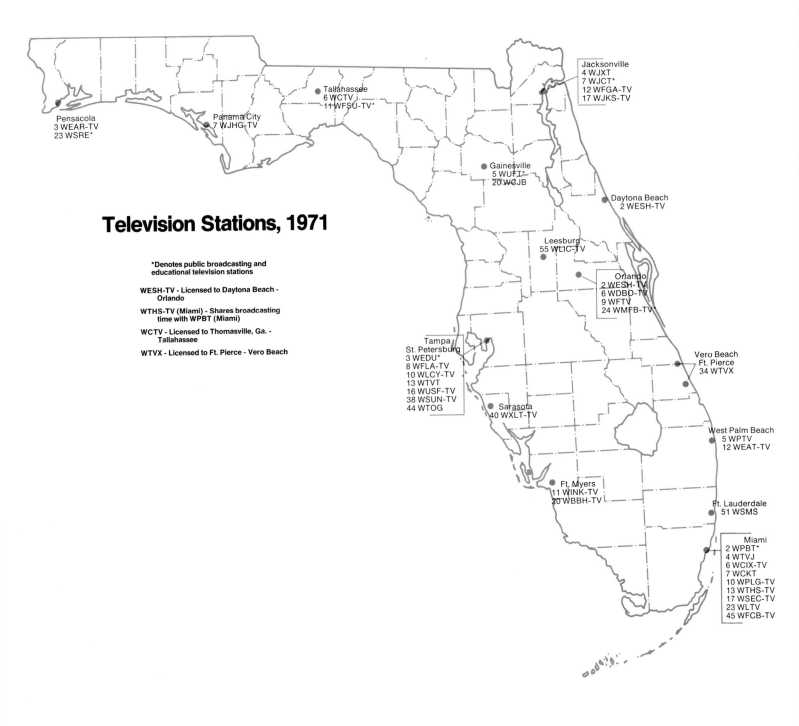

Television Stations, 1971

Pensacola
3 WEAR-TV
23 WSRE*

Panama City
7 WJHG-TV

Tallahassee
6 WCTV
11 WFSU-TV*

Jacksonville
4 WJXT*
7 WJCT*
12 WFGA-TV
17 WJKS-TV

Gainesville
5 WUFT*
20 WCJB

Daytona Beach
2 WESH-TV

Leesburg
55 WLIC-TV

Orlando
2 WESH-TV
6 WDBO-TV
9 WFTV
24 WMFB-TV

***Denotes public broadcasting and
educational television stations**

**WESH-TV - Licensed to Daytona Beach -
Orlando**

**WTHS-TV (Miami) - Shares broadcasting
time with WPBT (Miami)**

**WCTV - Licensed to Thomasville, Ga. -
Tallahassee**

WTVX - Licensed to Ft. Pierce - Vero Beach

Tampa
St. Petersburg
3 WEDU*
8 WFLA-TV
10 WLCY-TV
13 WTVT
16 WUSF-TV
38 WSUN-TV
44 WTOG

Sarasota
40 WXLT-TV

Vero Beach
Ft. Pierce
34 WTVX

West Palm Beach
5 WPTV
12 WEAT-TV

Ft. Myers
11 WINK-TV
20 WBBH-TV

Ft. Lauderdale
51 WSMS

Miami
2 WPBT*
4 WTVJ
6 WCIX-TV
7 WCKT
10 WPLG-TV
13 WTHS-TV
17 WSEC-TV
23 WLTV
45 WFCB-TV

Tourism and Recreation

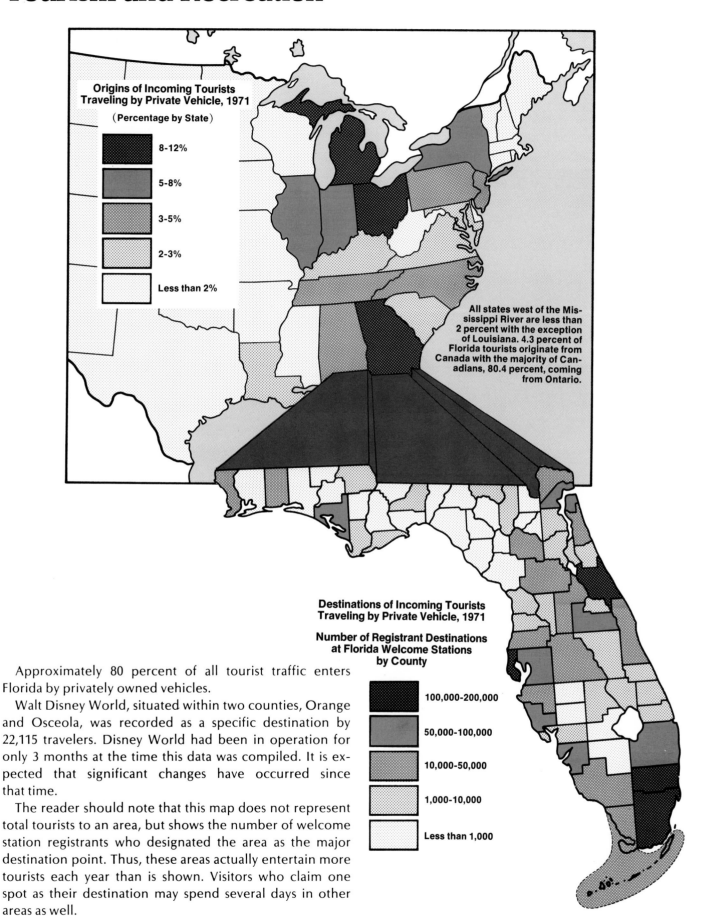

Origins of Incoming Tourists Traveling by Private Vehicle, 1971

(Percentage by State)

- 8-12%
- 5-8%
- 3-5%
- 2-3%
- Less than 2%

All states west of the Mississippi River are less than 2 percent with the exception of Louisiana. 4.3 percent of Florida tourists originate from Canada with the majority of Canadians, 80.4 percent, coming from Ontario.

Destinations of Incoming Tourists Traveling by Private Vehicle, 1971

Number of Registrant Destinations at Florida Welcome Stations by County

- 100,000-200,000
- 50,000-100,000
- 10,000-50,000
- 1,000-10,000
- Less than 1,000

Approximately 80 percent of all tourist traffic enters Florida by privately owned vehicles.

Walt Disney World, situated within two counties, Orange and Osceola, was recorded as a specific destination by 22,115 travelers. Disney World had been in operation for only 3 months at the time this data was compiled. It is expected that significant changes have occurred since that time.

The reader should note that this map does not represent total tourists to an area, but shows the number of welcome station registrants who designated the area as the major destination point. Thus, these areas actually entertain more tourists each year than is shown. Visitors who claim one spot as their destination may spend several days in other areas as well.

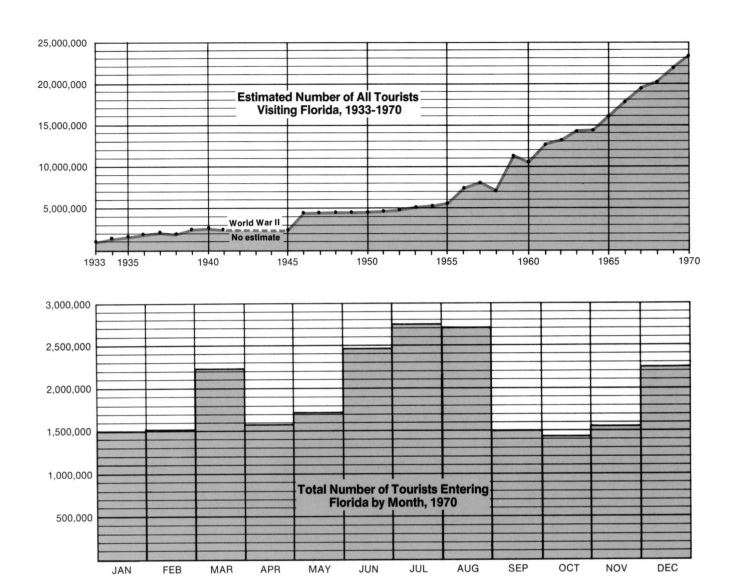

**Estimated Number of All Tourists
Visiting Florida, 1933-1970**

World War II
No estimate

**Total Number of Tourists Entering
Florida by Month, 1970**

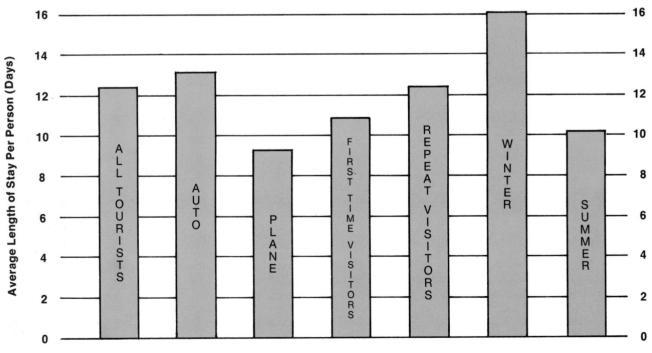

Estimated Length of Stay, 1970

Average Length of Stay Per Person (Days)

ALL TOURISTS

AUTO

PLANE

FIRST TIME VISITORS

REPEAT VISITORS

WINTER

SUMMER

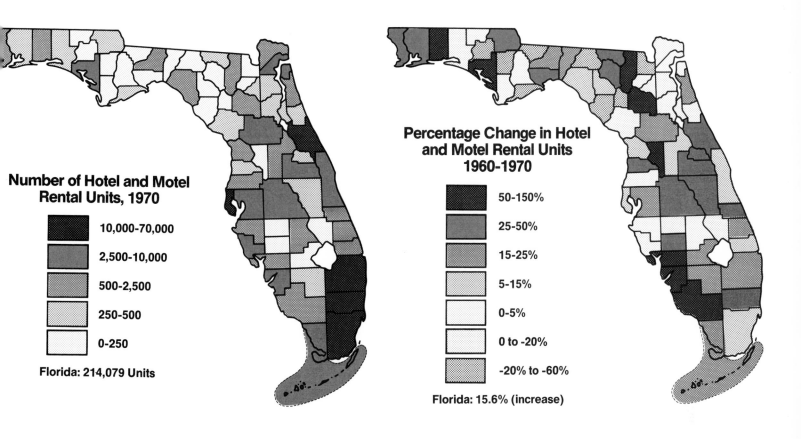

Number of Hotel and Motel Rental Units, 1970

■	10,000-70,000
▓	2,500-10,000
▒	500-2,500
░	250-500
□	0-250

Florida: 214,079 Units

Percentage Change in Hotel and Motel Rental Units 1960-1970

■	50-150%
▓	25-50%
▒	15-25%
░	5-15%
□	0-5%
□	0 to -20%
▒	-20% to -60%

Florida: 15.6% (increase)

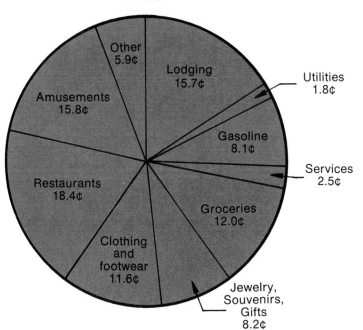

Division of Tourist Dollar 1968

Other 5.9¢
Lodging 15.7¢
Utilities 1.8¢
Amusements 15.8¢
Gasoline 8.1¢
Services 2.5¢
Restaurants 18.4¢
Groceries 12.0¢
Clothing and footwear 1.1.6¢
Jewelry, Souvenirs, Gifts 8.2¢

Tourists enjoy Florida fishing.

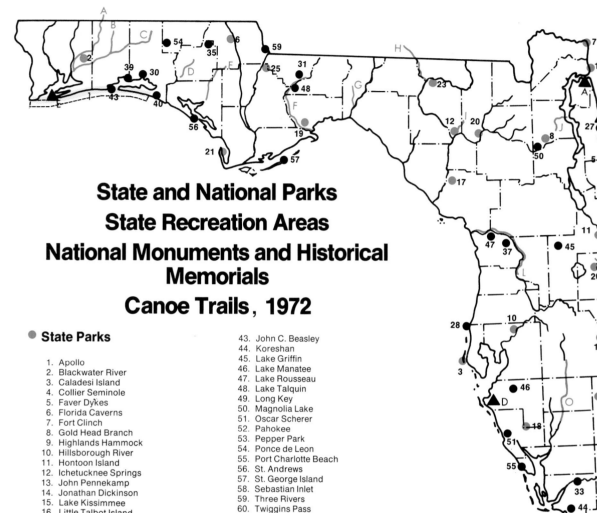

State and National Parks
State Recreation Areas
National Monuments and Historical Memorials
Canoe Trails, 1972

● State Parks

1. Apollo
2. Blackwater River
3. Caladesi Island
4. Collier Seminole
5. Faver Dykes
6. Florida Caverns
7. Fort Clinch
8. Gold Head Branch
9. Highlands Hammock
10. Hillsborough River
11. Hontoon Island
12. Ichetucknee Springs
13. John Pennekamp
14. Jonathan Dickinson
15. Lake Kissimmee
16. Little Talbot Island
17. Manatee Springs
18. Myakka River
19. Ochlockonee River
20. O'Leno
21. St. Joseph
22. St. Lucie Inlet
23. Suwannee River
24. Tomoka
25. Torreya
26. Wekiwa Springs

● State Recreation Areas

27. Anastasia
28. Anclote Key
29. Bahia Honda
30. Basin Bayou
31. Bear Creek
32. Blue Springs
33. Caloosahatchee River
34. Cape Florida
35. Falling Waters
36. Flagler Beach
37. Fort Cooper
38. Frank B. Butler
39. Fred Gannon Rocky Bayou
40. Grayton Beach
41. Grossman Hammock
42. Hugh Taylor Birch

43. John C. Beasley
44. Koreshan
45. Lake Griffin
46. Lake Manatee
47. Lake Rousseau
48. Lake Talquin
49. Long Key
50. Magnolia Lake
51. Oscar Scherer
52. Pahokee
53. Pepper Park
54. Ponce de Leon
55. Port Charlotte Beach
56. St. Andrews
57. St. George Island
58. Sebastian Inlet
59. Three Rivers
60. Twiggins Pass

▲ National Monuments and Historical Memorials

A. Fort Caroline
B. Castillo de San Marcos
C. Fort Matanzas
D. Fort DeSoto
E. Fort Pickens
F. Fort Jefferson

▢ National Parks

1. Gulf Islands National Seashore
2. Everglades National Park

〰 Canoe Trails

A. Blackwater River
B. Yellow River
C. Shoal River
D. Holmes Creek
E. Econfina River
F. Ochlockonee River
G. Wacissa River
H. Withlacoochee River
I. Ichetucknee River
J. Black Creek
K. Bulow Creek
L. Withlacoochee River
M. Wekiva River
N. Econlockhatchee River
O. Peace River
P. Loxahatchee River

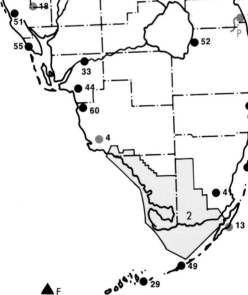

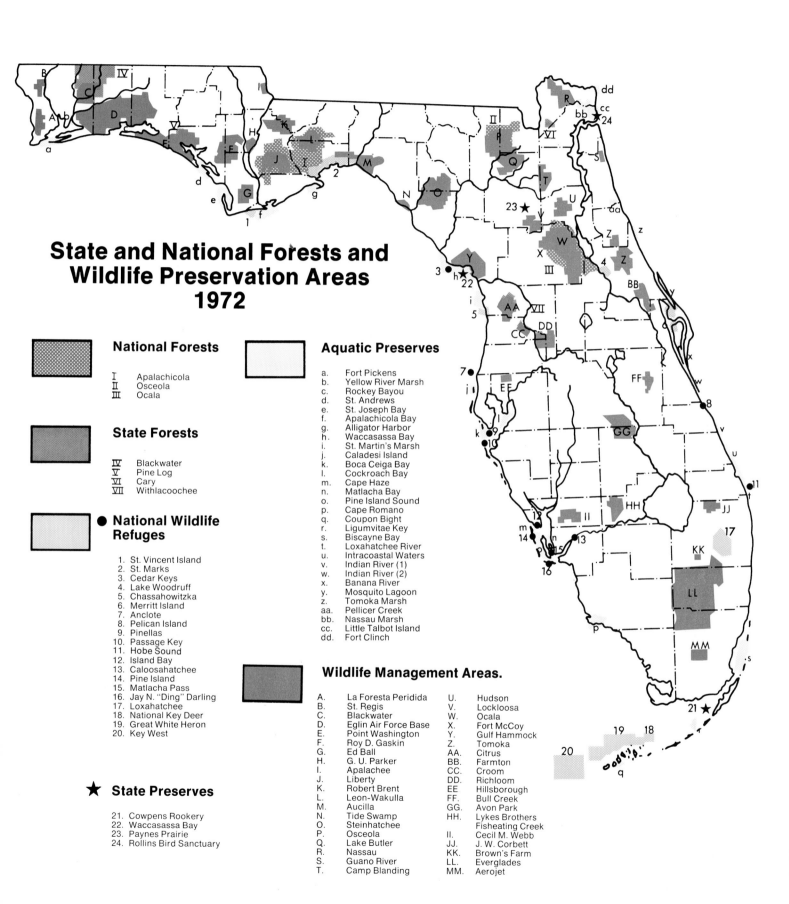

State and National Forests and Wildlife Preservation Areas 1972

National Forests

I   Apalachicola
II   Osceola
III   Ocala

State Forests

IV   Blackwater
V   Pine Log
VI   Cary
VII   Withlacoochee

● National Wildlife Refuges

1. St. Vincent Island
2. St. Marks
3. Cedar Keys
4. Lake Woodruff
5. Chassahowitzka
6. Merritt Island
7. Anclote
8. Pelican Island
9. Pinellas
10. Passage Key
11. Hobe Sound
12. Island Bay
13. Caloosahatchee
14. Pine Island
15. Matlacha Pass
16. Jay N. "Ding" Darling
17. Loxahatchee
18. National Key Deer
19. Great White Heron
20. Key West

★ State Preserves

21. Cowpens Rookery
22. Waccasassa Bay
23. Paynes Prairie
24. Rollins Bird Sanctuary

Aquatic Preserves

a.   Fort Pickens
b.   Yellow River Marsh
c.   Rockey Bayou
d.   St. Andrews
e.   St. Joseph Bay
f.   Apalachicola Bay
g.   Alligator Harbor
h.   Waccasassa Bay
i.   St. Martin's Marsh
j.   Caladesi Island
k.   Boca Ceiga Bay
l.   Cockroach Bay
m.   Cape Haze
n.   Matlacha Bay
o.   Pine Island Sound
p.   Cape Romano
q.   Coupon Bight
r.   Ligumvitae Key
s.   Biscayne Bay
t.   Loxahatchee River
u.   Intracoastal Waters
v.   Indian River (1)
w.   Indian River (2)
x.   Banana River
y.   Mosquito Lagoon
z.   Tomoka Marsh
aa.   Pellicer Creek
bb.   Nassau Marsh
cc.   Little Talbot Island
dd.   Fort Clinch

Wildlife Management Areas.

A.	La Foresta Peridida	U.	Hudson
B.	St. Regis	V.	Lockloosa
C.	Blackwater	W.	Ocala
D.	Eglin Air Force Base	X.	Fort McCoy
E.	Point Washington	Y.	Gulf Hammock
F.	Roy D. Gaskin	Z.	Tomoka
G.	Ed Ball	AA.	Citrus
H.	G. U. Parker	BB.	Farmton
I.	Apalachee	CC.	Croom
J.	Liberty	DD.	Richloom
K.	Robert Brent	EE.	Hillsborough
L.	Leon-Wakulla	FF.	Bull Creek
M.	Aucilla	GG.	Avon Park
N.	Tide Swamp	HH.	Lykes Brothers
O.	Steinhatchee		Fisheating Creek
P.	Osceola	II.	Cecil M. Webb
Q.	Lake Butler	JJ.	J. W. Corbett
R.	Nassau	KK.	Brown's Farm
S.	Guano River	LL.	Everglades
T.	Camp Blanding	MM.	Aerojet

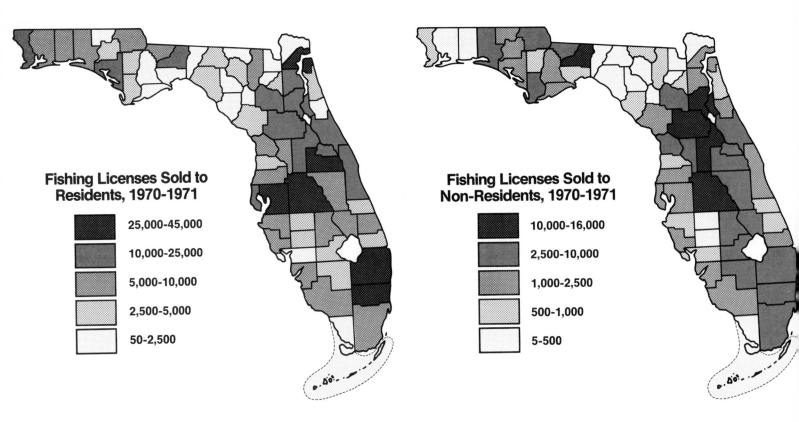

Fishing Licenses Sold to Residents, 1970-1971

- 25,000-45,000
- 10,000-25,000
- 5,000-10,000
- 2,500-5,000
- 50-2,500

Fishing Licenses Sold to Non-Residents, 1970-1971

- 10,000-16,000
- 2,500-10,000
- 1,000-2,500
- 500-1,000
- 5-500

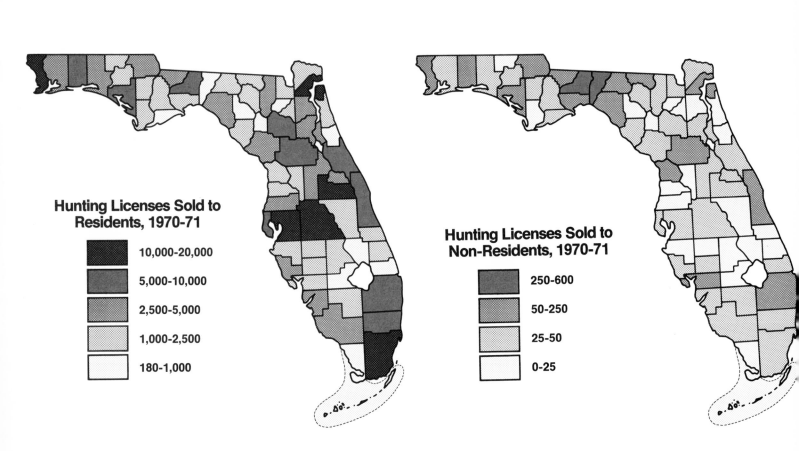

Hunting Licenses Sold to Residents, 1970-71

- 10,000-20,000
- 5,000-10,000
- 2,500-5,000
- 1,000-2,500
- 180-1,000

Hunting Licenses Sold to Non-Residents, 1970-71

- 250-600
- 50-250
- 25-50
- 0-25

Economic Activity

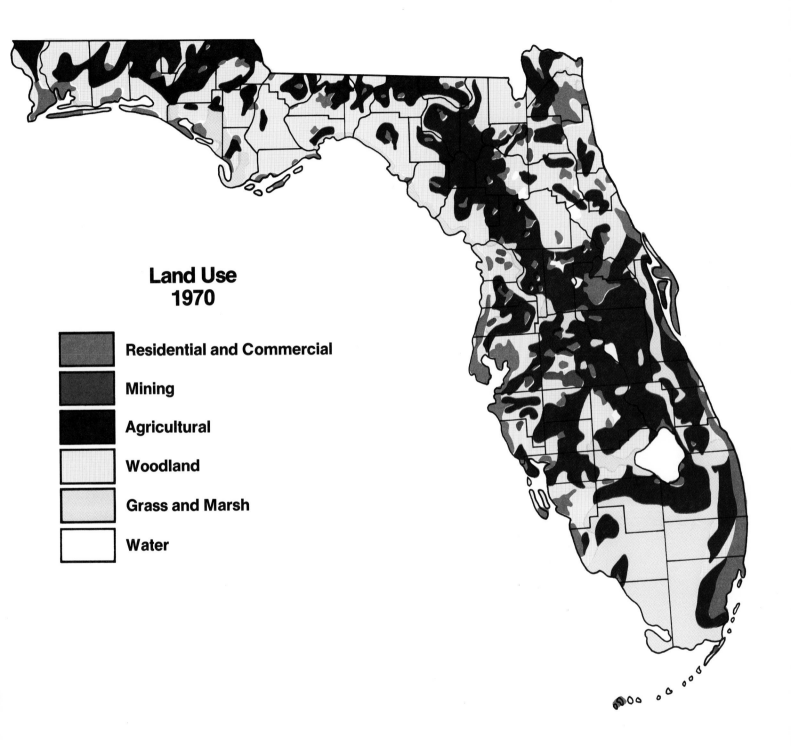

**Land Use
1970**

Residential and Commercial

Mining

Agricultural

Woodland

Grass and Marsh

Water

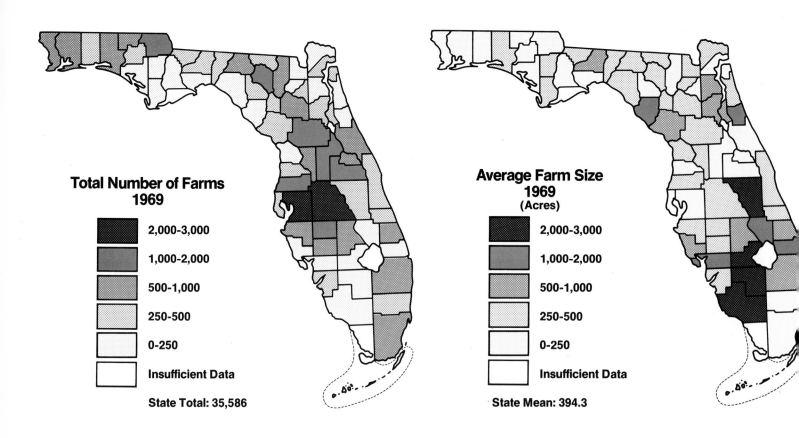

**Total Number of Farms
1969**

- 2,000-3,000
- 1,000-2,000
- 500-1,000
- 250-500
- 0-250
- Insufficient Data

State Total: 35,586

**Average Farm Size
1969**
(Acres)

- 2,000-3,000
- 1,000-2,000
- 500-1,000
- 250-500
- 0-250
- Insufficient Data

State Mean: 394.3

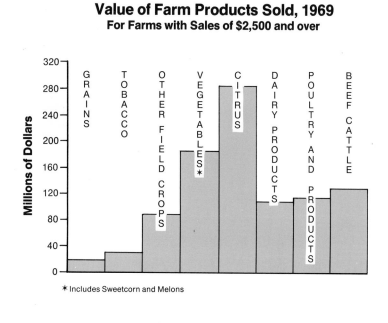

Value of Farm Products Sold, 1969
For Farms with Sales of $2,500 and over

GRAINS · TOBACCO · OTHER FIELD CROPS · VEGETABLES* · CITRUS · DAIRY PRODUCTS · POULTRY AND PRODUCTS · BEEF CATTLE

Millions of Dollars

* Includes Sweetcorn and Melons

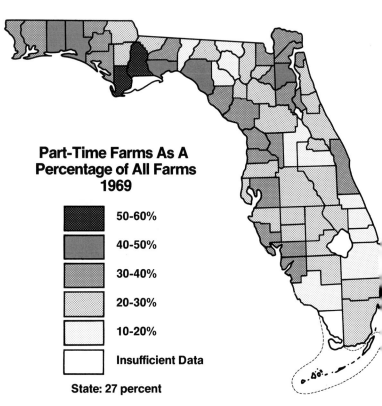

**Part-Time Farms As A
Percentage of All Farms
1969**

- 50-60%
- 40-50%
- 30-40%
- 20-30%
- 10-20%
- Insufficient Data

State: 27 percent

"Part-time farms" are classified by the Bureau of the Census as farms with a total value of farm products sold between $50 to $2,499 per year and a farm operator under 65 years of age who worked off the farm for 100 days or more in the census year.

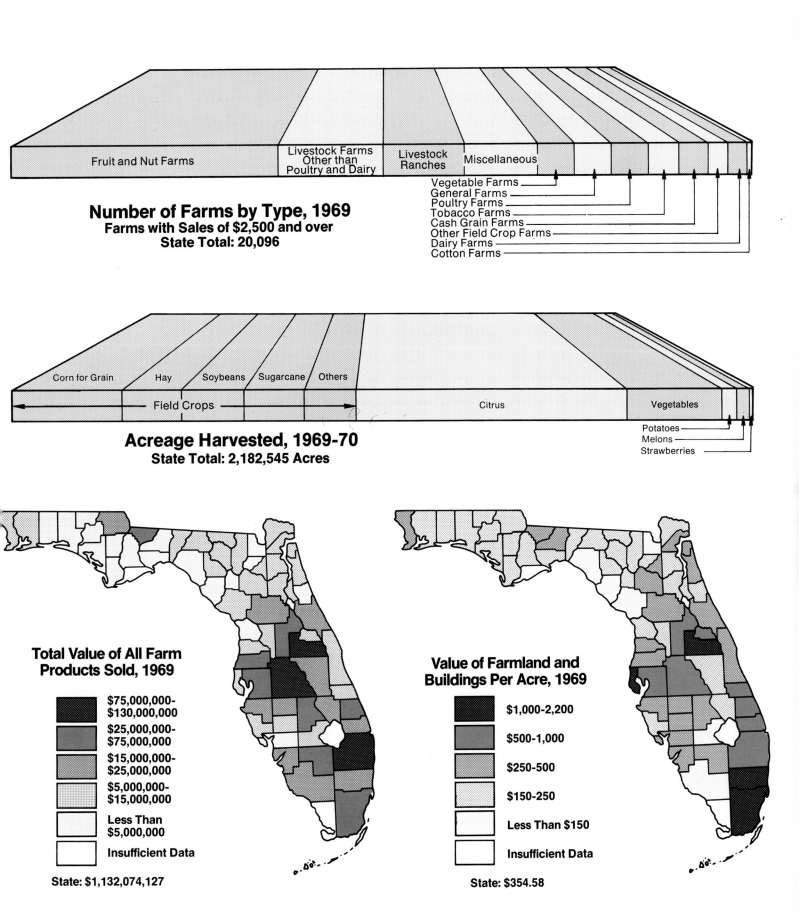

Number of Farms by Type, 1969
Farms with Sales of $2,500 and over
State Total: 20,096

Fruit and Nut Farms

Livestock Farms Other than Poultry and Dairy

Livestock Ranches

Miscellaneous

Vegetable Farms
General Farms
Poultry Farms
Tobacco Farms
Cash Grain Farms
Other Field Crop Farms
Dairy Farms
Cotton Farms

Acreage Harvested, 1969-70
State Total: 2,182,545 Acres

Corn for Grain   Hay   Soybeans   Sugarcane   Others

Field Crops

Citrus

Vegetables

Potatoes
Melons
Strawberries

Total Value of All Farm Products Sold, 1969

$75,000,000-$130,000,000

$25,000,000-$75,000,000

$15,000,000-$25,000,000

$5,000,000-$15,000,000

Less Than $5,000,000

Insufficient Data

State: $1,132,074,127

Value of Farmland and Buildings Per Acre, 1969

$1,000-2,200

$500-1,000

$250-500

$150-250

Less Than $150

Insufficient Data

State: $354.58

81

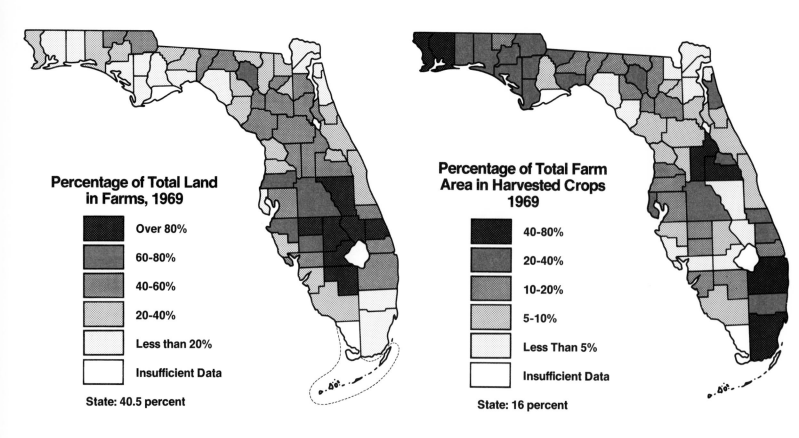

Percentage of Total Land in Farms, 1969

- Over 80%
- 60-80%
- 40-60%
- 20-40%
- Less than 20%
- Insufficient Data

State: 40.5 percent

Percentage of Total Farm Area in Harvested Crops 1969

- 40-80%
- 20-40%
- 10-20%
- 5-10%
- Less Than 5%
- Insufficient Data

State: 16 percent

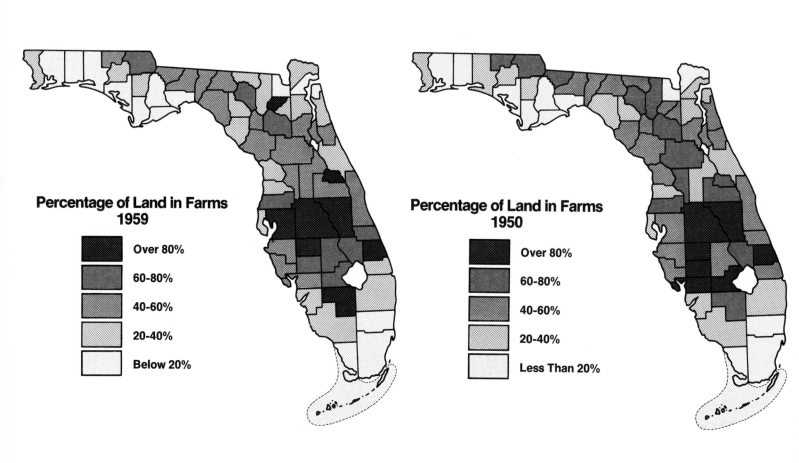

Percentage of Land in Farms 1959

- Over 80%
- 60-80%
- 40-60%
- 20-40%
- Below 20%

Percentage of Land in Farms 1950

- Over 80%
- 60-80%
- 40-60%
- 20-40%
- Less Than 20%

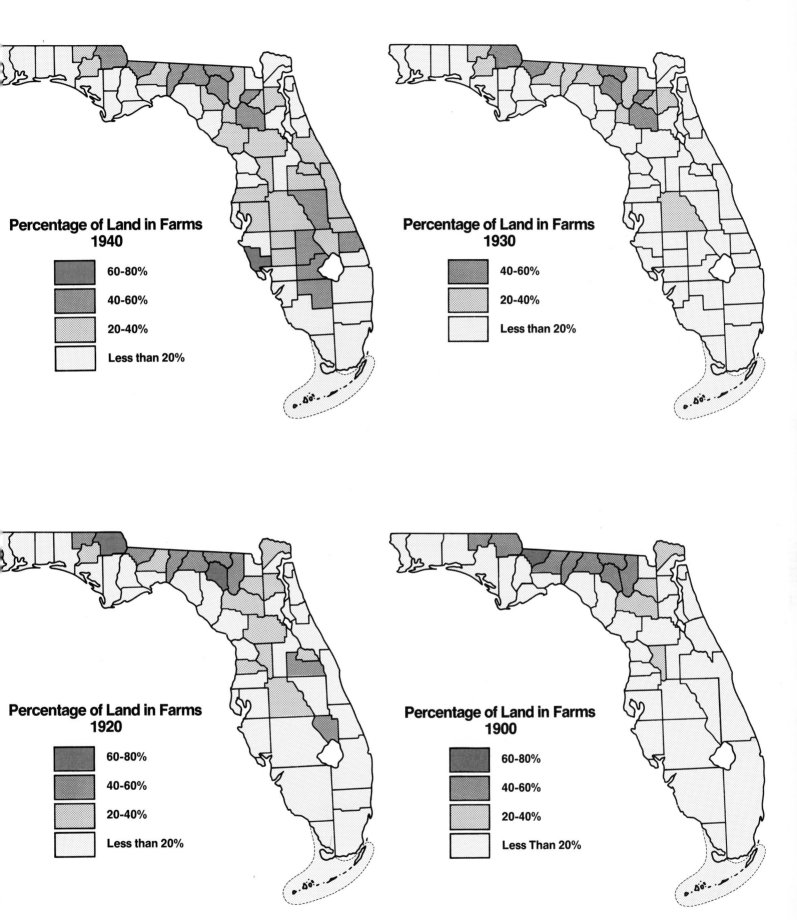

**Percentage of Land in Farms
1940**

- 60-80%
- 40-60%
- 20-40%
- Less than 20%

**Percentage of Land in Farms
1930**

- 40-60%
- 20-40%
- Less than 20%

**Percentage of Land in Farms
1920**

- 60-80%
- 40-60%
- 20-40%
- Less than 20%

**Percentage of Land in Farms
1900**

- 60-80%
- 40-60%
- 20-40%
- Less Than 20%

Refer to historical maps on page 109 for county names.

Harvested Vegetable and Small Fruit Acreage, 1969

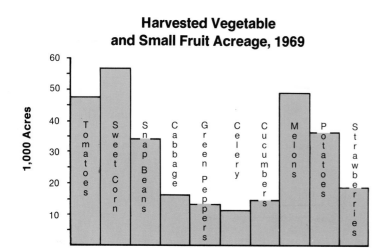

1,000 Acres

Tomatoes, Sweet Corn, Snap Beans, Cabbage, Green Peppers, Celery, Cucumbers, Melons, Potatoes, Strawberries

Vegetable, Potato, Berry and Melon Acreage, 1969

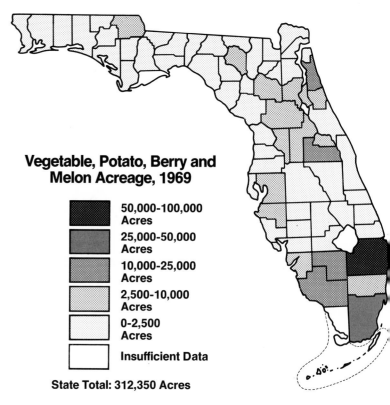

- 50,000-100,000 Acres
- 25,000-50,000 Acres
- 10,000-25,000 Acres
- 2,500-10,000 Acres
- 0-2,500 Acres
- Insufficient Data

State Total: 312,350 Acres

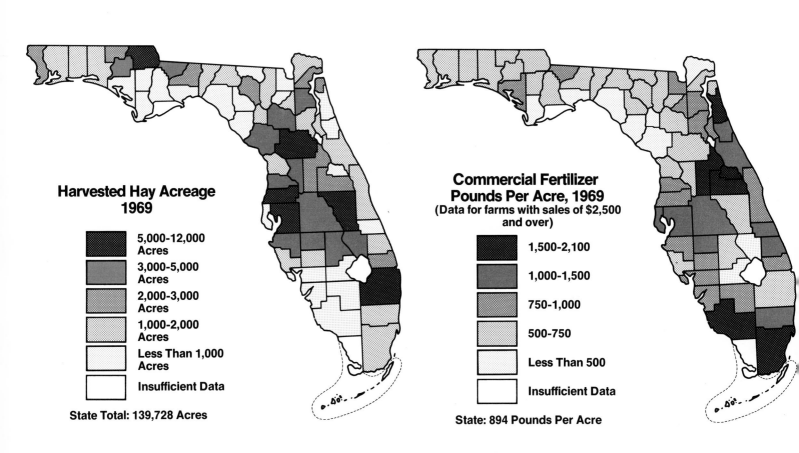

Harvested Hay Acreage 1969

- 5,000-12,000 Acres
- 3,000-5,000 Acres
- 2,000-3,000 Acres
- 1,000-2,000 Acres
- Less Than 1,000 Acres
- Insufficient Data

State Total: 139,728 Acres

Commercial Fertilizer Pounds Per Acre, 1969
(Data for farms with sales of $2,500 and over)

- 1,500-2,100
- 1,000-1,500
- 750-1,000
- 500-750
- Less Than 500
- Insufficient Data

State: 894 Pounds Per Acre

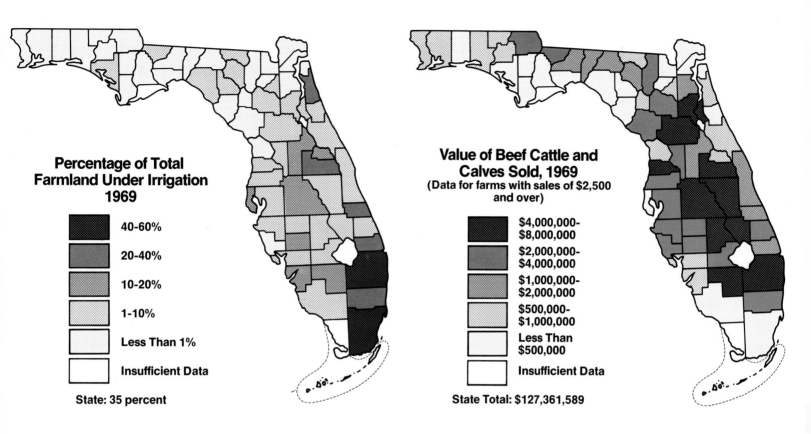

Percentage of Total Farmland Under Irrigation 1969

■	40-60%
▨	20-40%
▨	10-20%
▨	1-10%
▨	Less Than 1%
□	Insufficient Data

State: 35 percent

Value of Beef Cattle and Calves Sold, 1969
(Data for farms with sales of $2,500 and over)

■	$4,000,000-$8,000,000
▨	$2,000,000-$4,000,000
▨	$1,000,000-$2,000,000
▨	$500,000-$1,000,000
▨	Less Than $500,000
□	Insufficient Data

State Total: $127,361,589

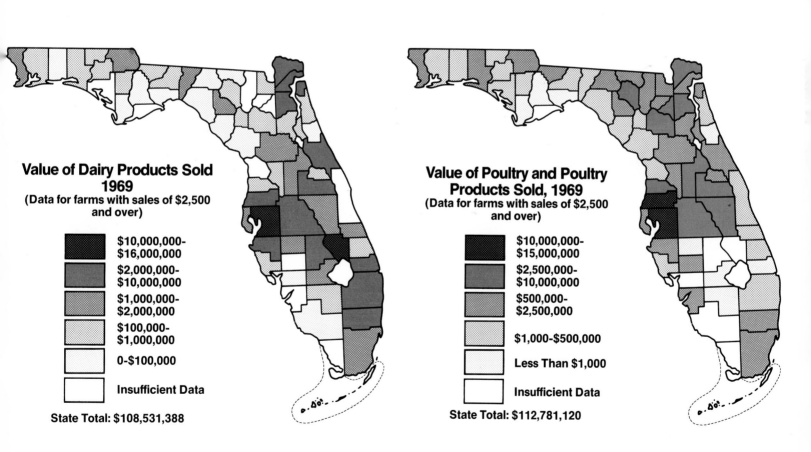

Value of Dairy Products Sold 1969
(Data for farms with sales of $2,500 and over)

■	$10,000,000-$16,000,000
▨	$2,000,000-$10,000,000
▨	$1,000,000-$2,000,000
▨	$100,000-$1,000,000
▨	0-$100,000
□	Insufficient Data

State Total: $108,531,388

Value of Poultry and Poultry Products Sold, 1969
(Data for farms with sales of $2,500 and over)

■	$10,000,000-$15,000,000
▨	$2,500,000-$10,000,000
▨	$500,000-$2,500,000
▨	$1,000-$500,000
▨	Less Than $1,000
□	Insufficient Data

State Total: $112,781,120

Citrus Production 1945-46 to 1970-71

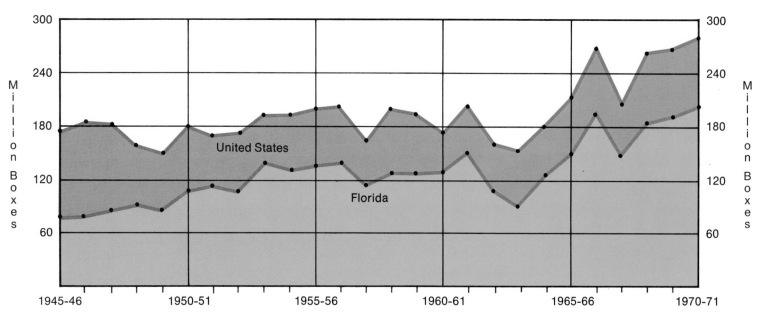

Citrus arrives at processing plant, Apopka.

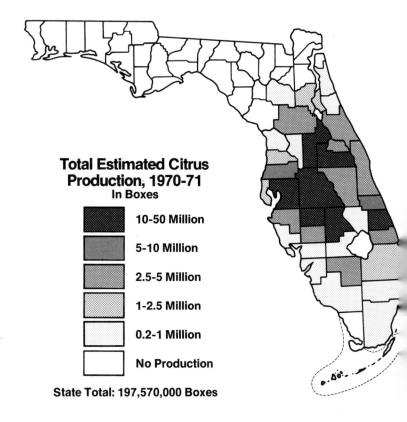

Total Estimated Citrus Production, 1970-71
In Boxes

- 10-50 Million
- 5-10 Million
- 2.5-5 Million
- 1-2.5 Million
- 0.2-1 Million
- No Production

State Total: 197,570,000 Boxes

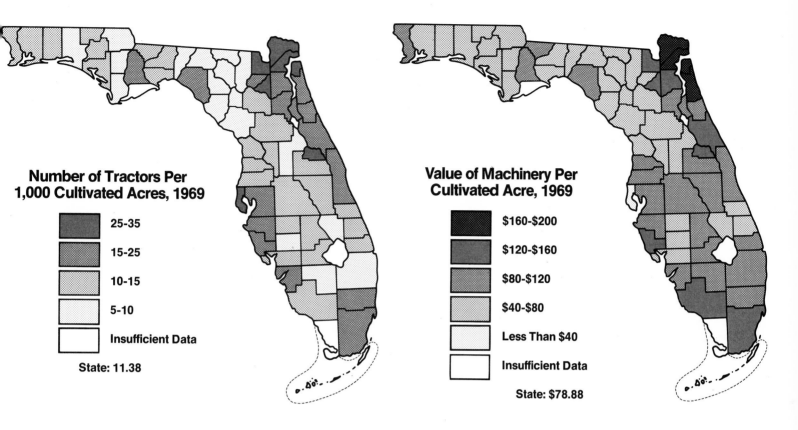

**Number of Tractors Per
1,000 Cultivated Acres, 1969**

- 25-35
- 15-25
- 10-15
- 5-10
- Insufficient Data

State: 11.38

**Value of Machinery Per
Cultivated Acre, 1969**

- $160-$200
- $120-$160
- $80-$120
- $40-$80
- Less Than $40
- Insufficient Data

State: $78.88

Farm Production Expenditures, 1969
State Total: $997,989,436

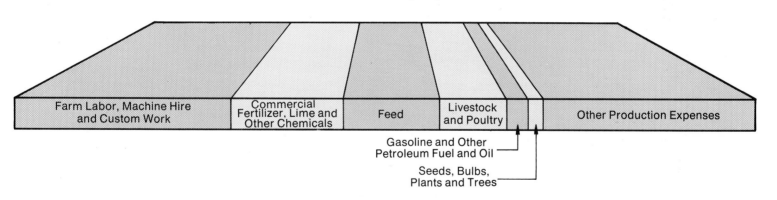

Farm Labor, Machine Hire and Custom Work

Commercial Fertilizer, Lime and Other Chemicals

Feed

Livestock and Poultry

Other Production Expenses

Gasoline and Other
Petroleum Fuel and Oil

Seeds, Bulbs,
Plants and Trees

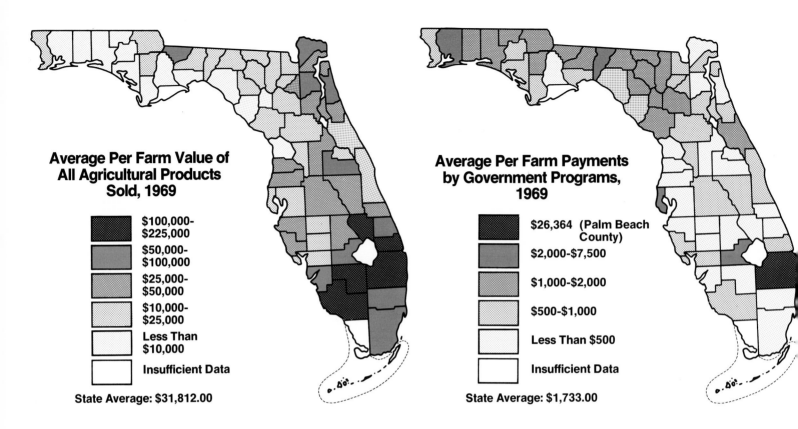

Average Per Farm Value of All Agricultural Products Sold, 1969

- $100,000-$225,000
- $50,000-$100,000
- $25,000-$50,000
- $10,000-$25,000
- Less Than $10,000
- Insufficient Data

State Average: $31,812.00

Average Per Farm Payments by Government Programs, 1969

- $26,364 (Palm Beach County)
- $2,000-$7,500
- $1,000-$2,000
- $500-$1,000
- Less Than $500
- Insufficient Data

State Average: $1,733.00

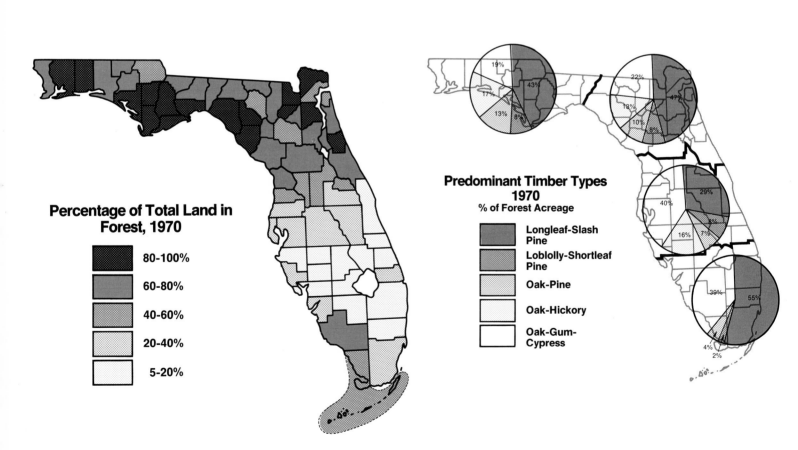

Percentage of Total Land in Forest, 1970

- 80-100%
- 60-80%
- 40-60%
- 20-40%
- 5-20%

Predominant Timber Types 1970
% of Forest Acreage

- Longleaf-Slash Pine
- Loblolly-Shortleaf Pine
- Oak-Pine
- Oak-Hickory
- Oak-Gum-Cypress

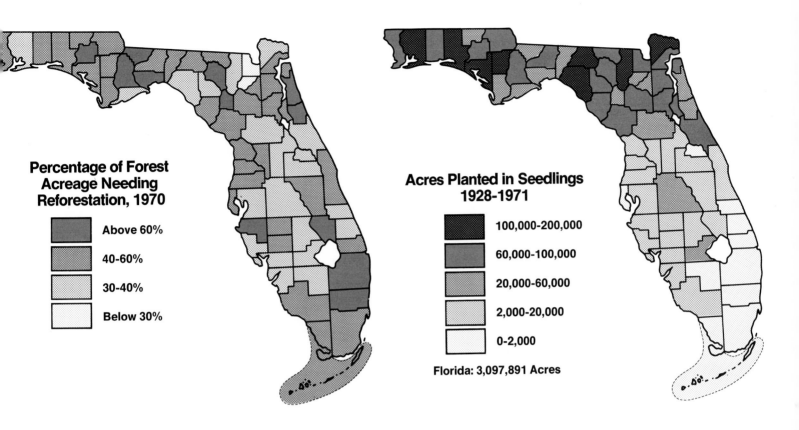

Percentage of Forest Acreage Needing Reforestation, 1970

- Above 60%
- 40-60%
- 30-40%
- Below 30%

Acres Planted in Seedlings 1928-1971

- 100,000-200,000
- 60,000-100,000
- 20,000-60,000
- 2,000-20,000
- 0-2,000

Florida: 3,097,891 Acres

Pine Seedlings Planted, 1951-1971

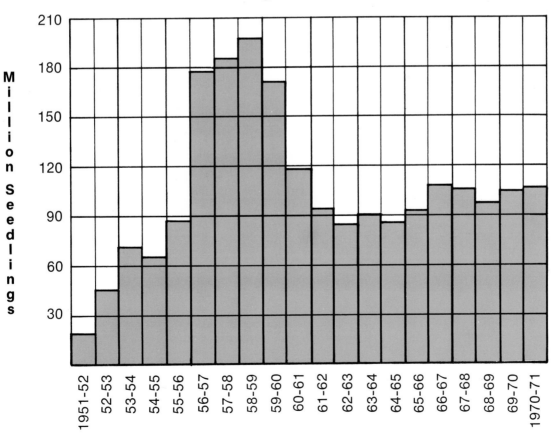

Million Seedlings

Ownership of Commercial Forest Areas, 1970

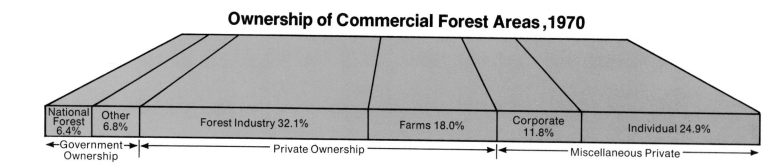

| National Forest 6.4% | Other 6.8% | Forest Industry 32.1% | Farms 18.0% | Corporate 11.8% | Individual 24.9% |

←Government→ Ownership | ←————— Private Ownership —————→ | ←——— Miscellaneous Private ———→

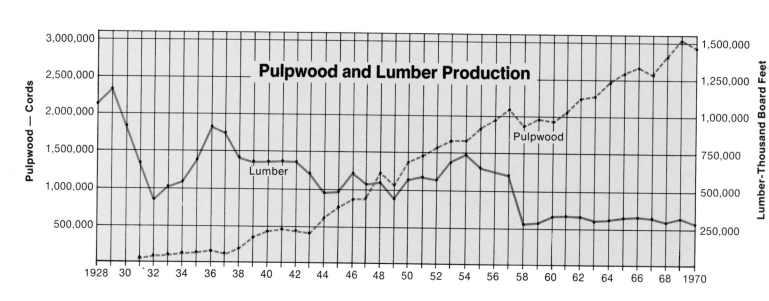

Pulpwood and Lumber Production

Pulpwood — Cords (left axis): 3,000,000 / 2,500,000 / 2,000,000 / 1,500,000 / 1,000,000 / 500,000

Lumber — Thousand Board Feet (right axis): 1,500,000 / 1,250,000 / 1,000,000 / 750,000 / 500,000 / 250,000

1928 30 '32 34 36 38 40 42 44 46 48 50 52 54 56 58 60 62 64 66 68 1970

Lumber
Pulpwood

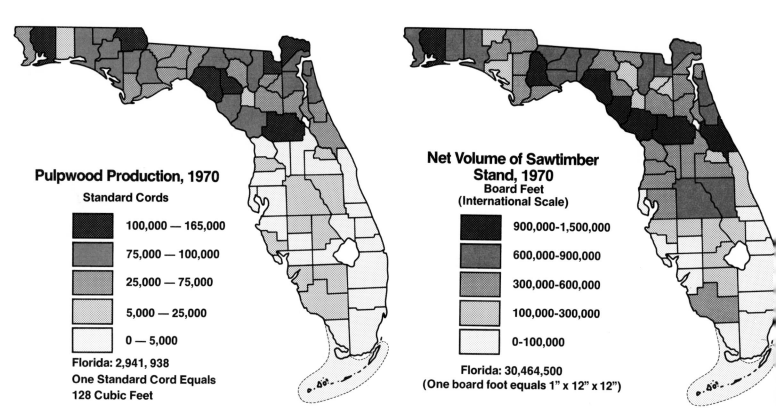

Pulpwood Production, 1970
Standard Cords

- 100,000 — 165,000
- 75,000 — 100,000
- 25,000 — 75,000
- 5,000 — 25,000
- 0 — 5,000

Florida: 2,941,938
One Standard Cord Equals
128 Cubic Feet

Net Volume of Sawtimber Stand, 1970
Board Feet (International Scale)

- 900,000-1,500,000
- 600,000-900,000
- 300,000-600,000
- 100,000-300,000
- 0-100,000

Florida: 30,464,500
(One board foot equals 1" x 12" x 12")

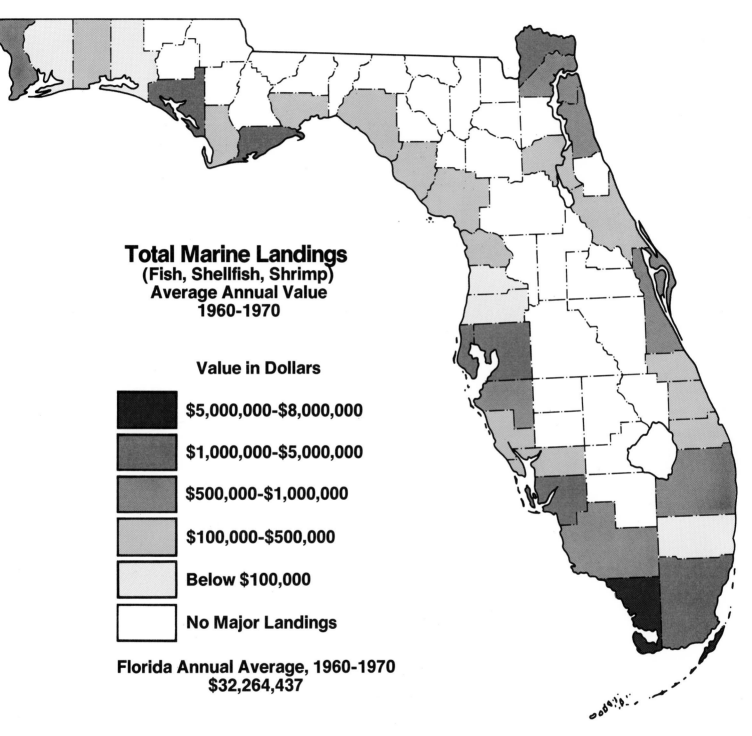

Total Marine Landings
(Fish, Shellfish, Shrimp)
Average Annual Value
1960-1970

Value in Dollars

$5,000,000-$8,000,000

$1,000,000-$5,000,000

$500,000-$1,000,000

$100,000-$500,000

Below $100,000

No Major Landings

Florida Annual Average, 1960-1970
$32,264,437

Note: Sources of data for Commercial Fishing combined values of fish catches for Dixie and Taylor Counties, and also for Pasco and Hernando Counties. Values shown on these maps are combined values in both instances.

A shrimp catch from the Gulf of Mexico

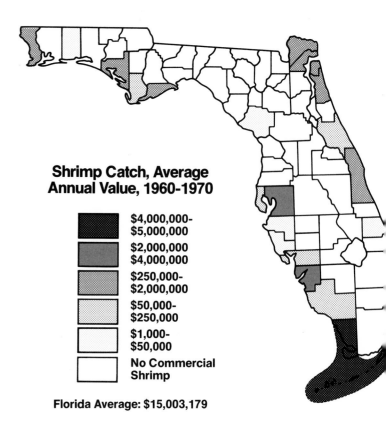

Shrimp Catch, Average Annual Value, 1960-1970

■	$4,000,000-$5,000,000
■	$2,000,000-$4,000,000
▨	$250,000-$2,000,000
▨	$50,000-$250,000
□	$1,000-$50,000
□	No Commercial Shrimp

Florida Average: $15,003,179

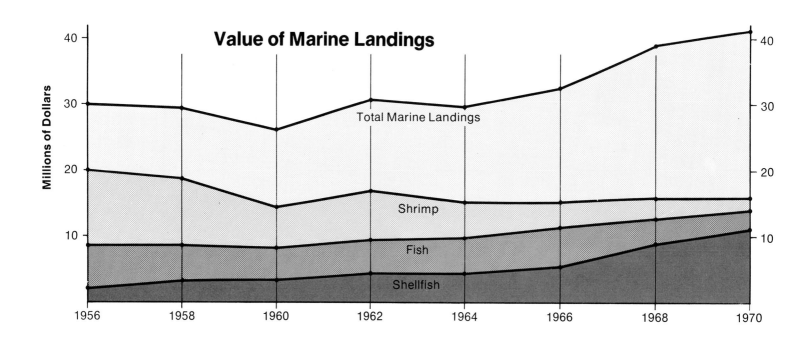

Value of Marine Landings

Total Marine Landings

Shrimp

Fish

Shellfish

Millions of Dollars

1956 1958 1960 1962 1964 1966 1968 1970

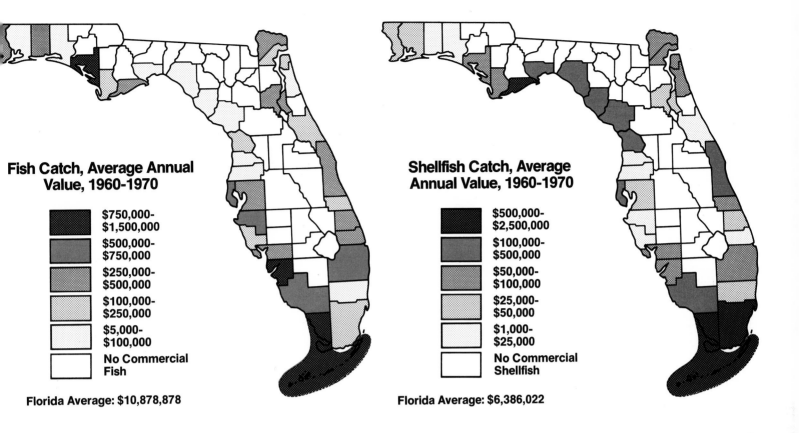

Fish Catch, Average Annual Value, 1960-1970

- $750,000-$1,500,000
- $500,000-$750,000
- $250,000-$500,000
- $100,000-$250,000
- $5,000-$100,000
- No Commercial Fish

Florida Average: $10,878,878

Shellfish Catch, Average Annual Value, 1960-1970

- $500,000-$2,500,000
- $100,000-$500,000
- $50,000-$100,000
- $25,000-$50,000
- $1,000-$25,000
- No Commercial Shellfish

Florida Average: $6,386,022

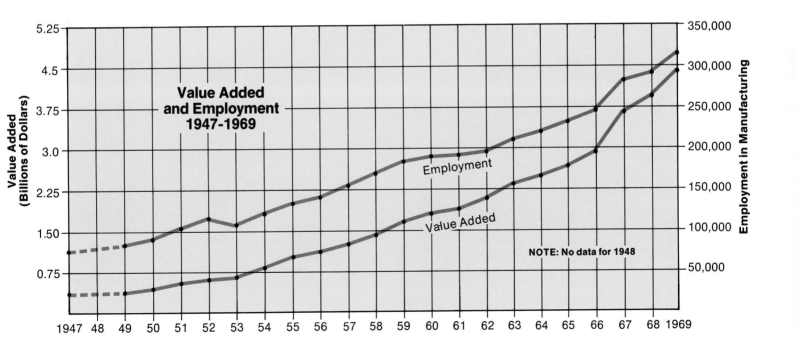

Value Added and Employment 1947-1969

Value Added (Billions of Dollars)

Employment in Manufacturing

Employment

Value Added

NOTE: No data for 1948

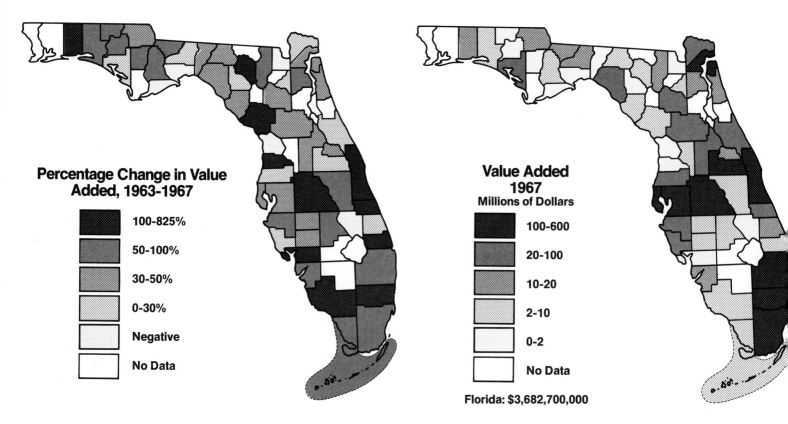

Percentage Change in Value Added, 1963-1967

- 100-825%
- 50-100%
- 30-50%
- 0-30%
- Negative
- No Data

Value Added
1967
Millions of Dollars

- 100-600
- 20-100
- 10-20
- 2-10
- 0-2
- No Data

Florida: $3,682,700,000

Until 1956 value added by manufacturing was derived by subtracting production costs from the value of shipments of manufactured goods. In subsequent years the figure has been adjusted to include value added by merchandising and net change in value of inventories.

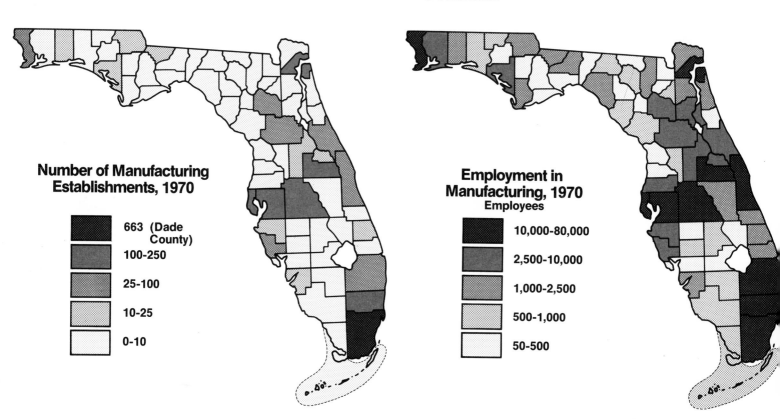

Number of Manufacturing Establishments, 1970

- 663 (Dade County)
- 100-250
- 25-100
- 10-25
- 0-10

Employment in Manufacturing, 1970
Employees

- 10,000-80,000
- 2,500-10,000
- 1,000-2,500
- 500-1,000
- 50-500

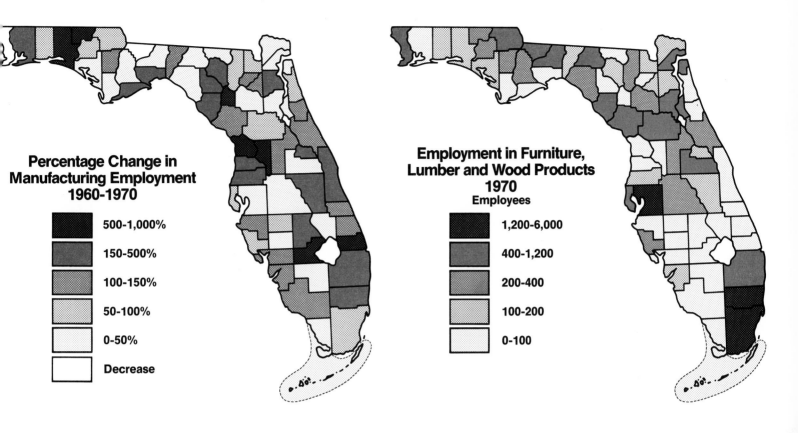

Percentage Change in Manufacturing Employment 1960-1970

- 500-1,000%
- 150-500%
- 100-150%
- 50-100%
- 0-50%
- Decrease

Employment in Furniture, Lumber and Wood Products 1970
Employees

- 1,200-6,000
- 400-1,200
- 200-400
- 100-200
- 0-100

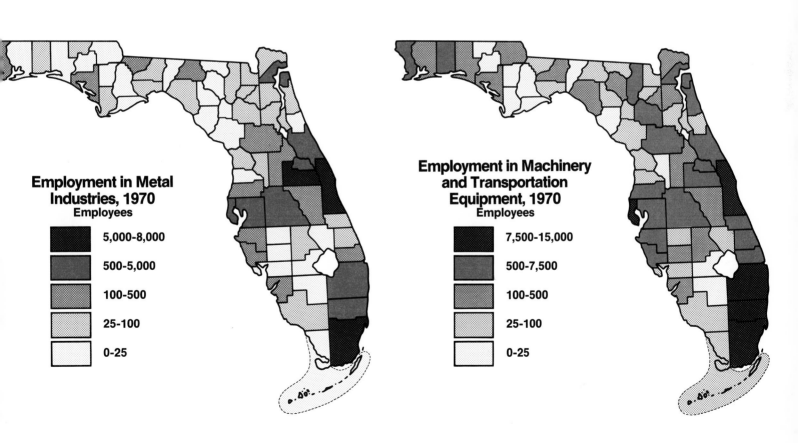

Employment in Metal Industries, 1970
Employees

- 5,000-8,000
- 500-5,000
- 100-500
- 25-100
- 0-25

Employment in Machinery and Transportation Equipment, 1970
Employees

- 7,500-15,000
- 500-7,500
- 100-500
- 25-100
- 0-25

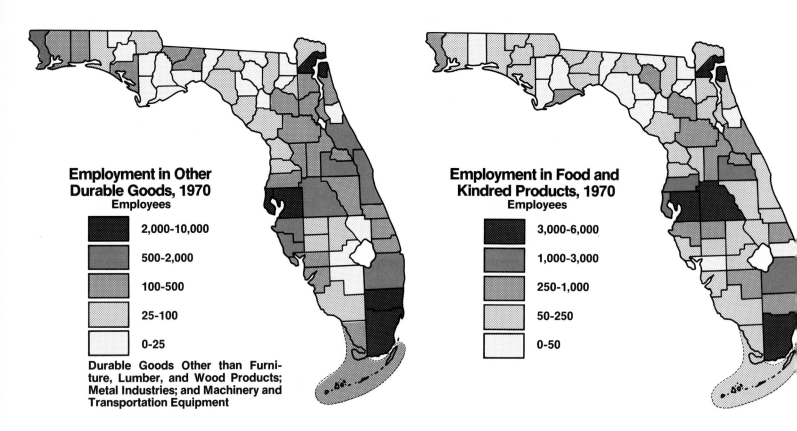

Employment in Other Durable Goods, 1970
Employees

■	2,000-10,000
▦	500-2,000
▦	100-500
▦	25-100
□	0-25

Durable Goods Other than Furniture, Lumber, and Wood Products; Metal Industries; and Machinery and Transportation Equipment

Employment in Food and Kindred Products, 1970
Employees

■	3,000-6,000
▦	1,000-3,000
▦	250-1,000
▦	50-250
▦	0-50

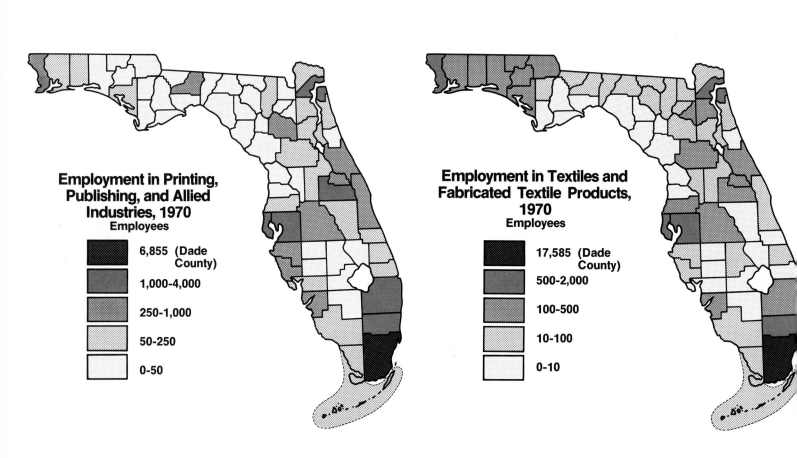

Employment in Printing, Publishing, and Allied Industries, 1970
Employees

■	6,855 (Dade County)
▦	1,000-4,000
▦	250-1,000
▦	50-250
□	0-50

Employment in Textiles and Fabricated Textile Products, 1970
Employees

■	17,585 (Dade County)
▦	500-2,000
▦	100-500
▦	10-100
□	0-10

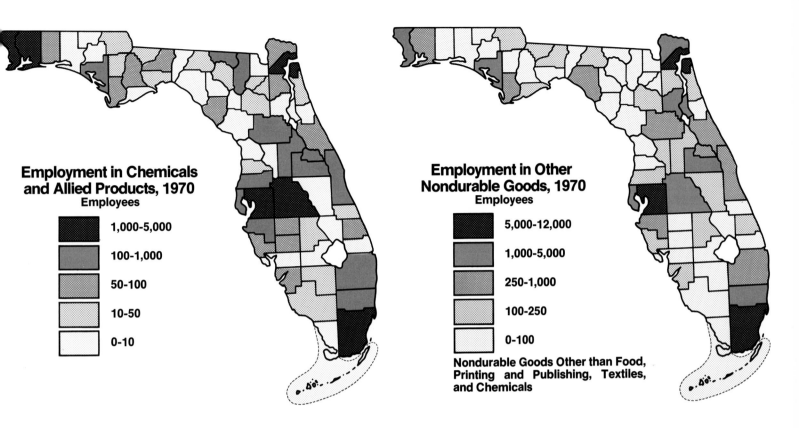

Employment in Chemicals and Allied Products, 1970
Employees

- 1,000-5,000
- 100-1,000
- 50-100
- 10-50
- 0-10

Employment in Other Nondurable Goods, 1970
Employees

- 5,000-12,000
- 1,000-5,000
- 250-1,000
- 100-250
- 0-100

Nondurable Goods Other than Food, Printing and Publishing, Textiles, and Chemicals

Phosphate storage in central Florida

Employment, 1970

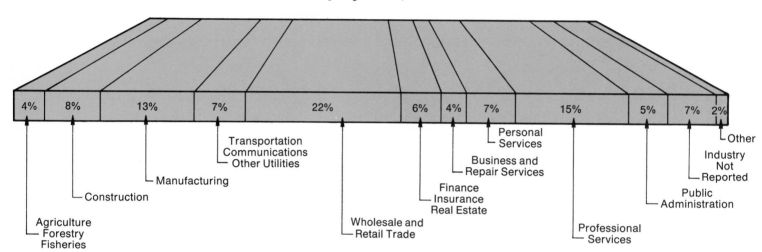

Employment, 1970

4% 8% 13% 7% 22% 6% 4% 7% 15% 5% 7% 2%

Agriculture Forestry Fisheries

Construction

Manufacturing

Transportation Communications Other Utilities

Wholesale and Retail Trade

Finance Insurance Real Estate

Business and Repair Services

Personal Services

Professional Services

Public Administration

Industry Not Reported

Other

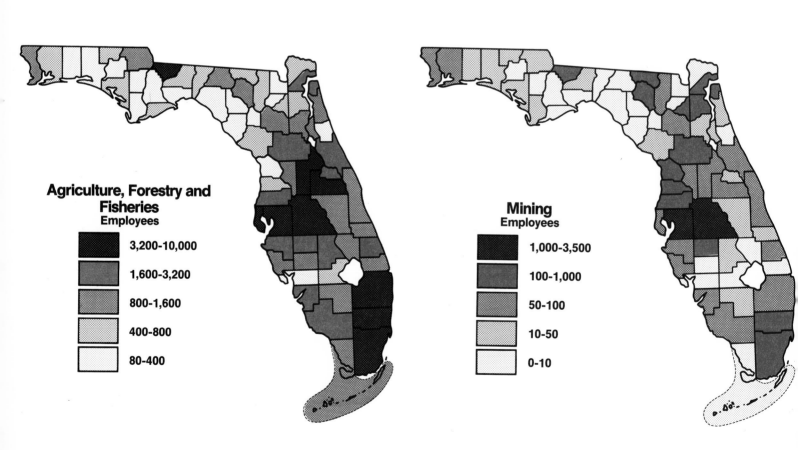

Agriculture, Forestry and Fisheries
Employees

	3,200-10,000
	1,600-3,200
	800-1,600
	400-800
	80-400

Mining
Employees

	1,000-3,500
	100-1,000
	50-100
	10-50
	0-10

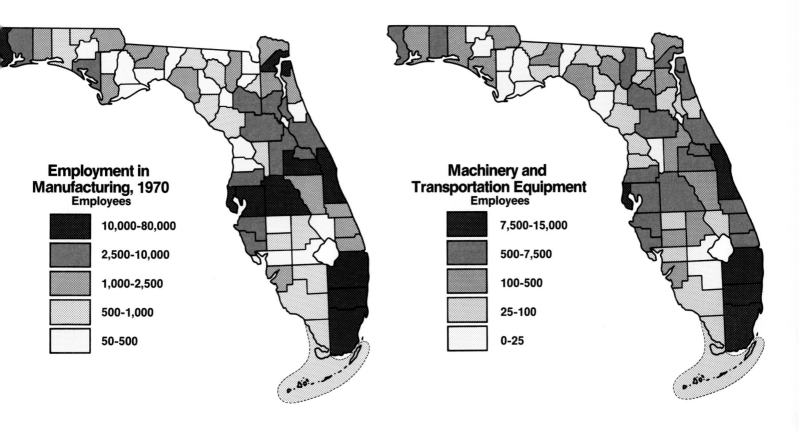

**Employment in
Manufacturing, 1970**
Employees

- 10,000-80,000
- 2,500-10,000
- 1,000-2,500
- 500-1,000
- 50-500

**Machinery and
Transportation Equipment**
Employees

- 7,500-15,000
- 500-7,500
- 100-500
- 25-100
- 0-25

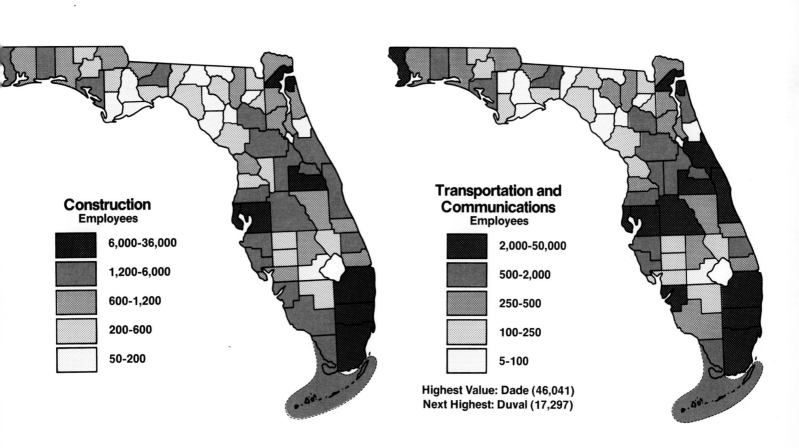

Construction
Employees

- 6,000-36,000
- 1,200-6,000
- 600-1,200
- 200-600
- 50-200

**Transportation and
Communications**
Employees

- 2,000-50,000
- 500-2,000
- 250-500
- 100-250
- 5-100

**Highest Value: Dade (46,041)
Next Highest: Duval (17,297)**

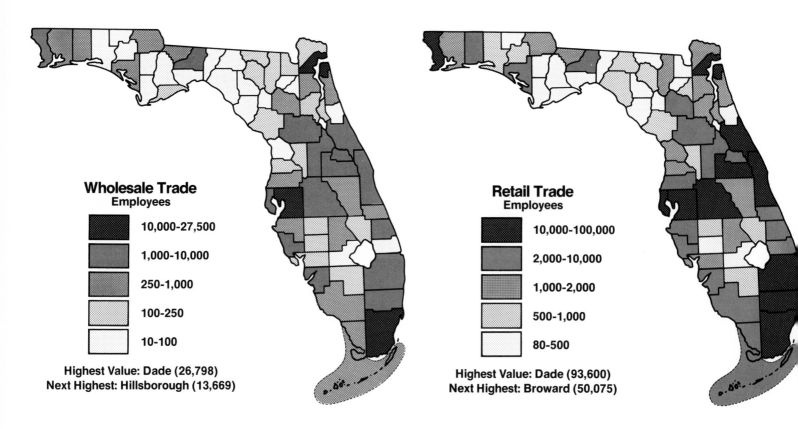

Wholesale Trade
Employees

- 10,000-27,500
- 1,000-10,000
- 250-1,000
- 100-250
- 10-100

Highest Value: Dade (26,798)
Next Highest: Hillsborough (13,669)

Retail Trade
Employees

- 10,000-100,000
- 2,000-10,000
- 1,000-2,000
- 500-1,000
- 80-500

Highest Value: Dade (93,600)
Next Highest: Broward (50,075)

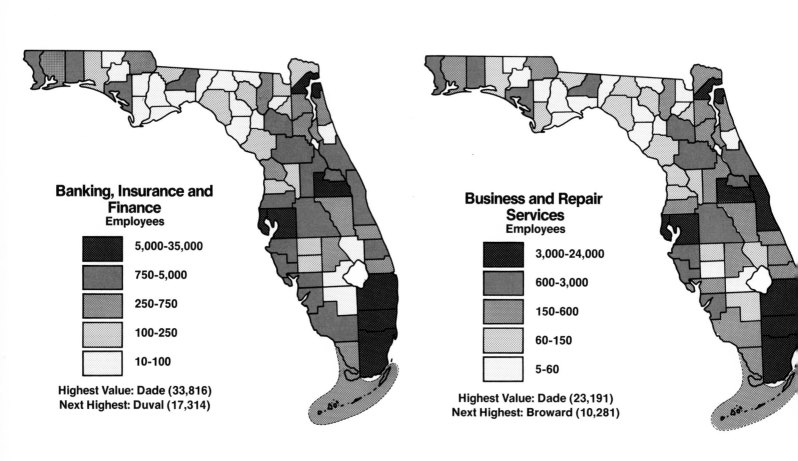

Banking, Insurance and Finance
Employees

- 5,000-35,000
- 750-5,000
- 250-750
- 100-250
- 10-100

Highest Value: Dade (33,816)
Next Highest: Duval (17,314)

Business and Repair Services
Employees

- 3,000-24,000
- 600-3,000
- 150-600
- 60-150
- 5-60

Highest Value: Dade (23,191)
Next Highest: Broward (10,281)

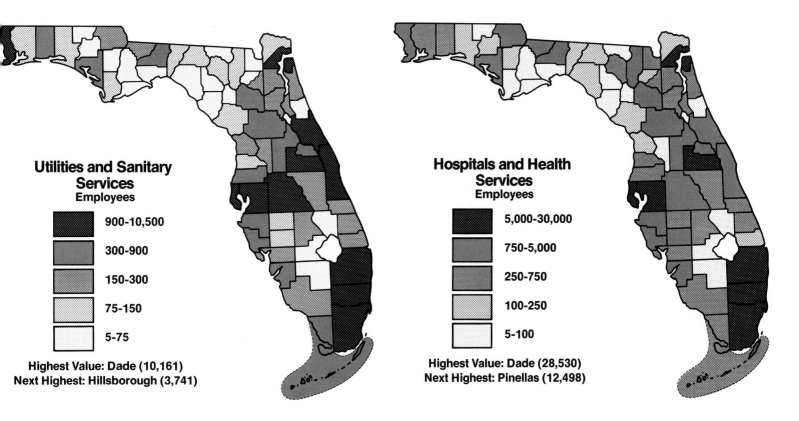

Utilities and Sanitary Services
Employees

■	900-10,500
▨	300-900
▨	150-300
░	75-150
□	5-75

Highest Value: Dade (10,161)
Next Highest: Hillsborough (3,741)

Hospitals and Health Services
Employees

■	5,000-30,000
▨	750-5,000
▨	250-750
░	100-250
□	5-100

Highest Value: Dade (28,530)
Next Highest: Pinellas (12,498)

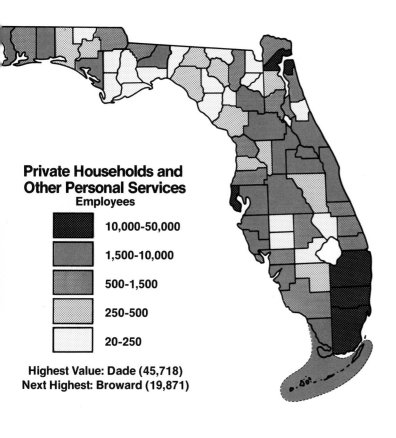

Private Households and Other Personal Services
Employees

■	10,000-50,000
▨	1,500-10,000
▨	500-1,500
░	250-500
□	20-250

Highest Value: Dade (45,718)
Next Highest: Broward (19,871)

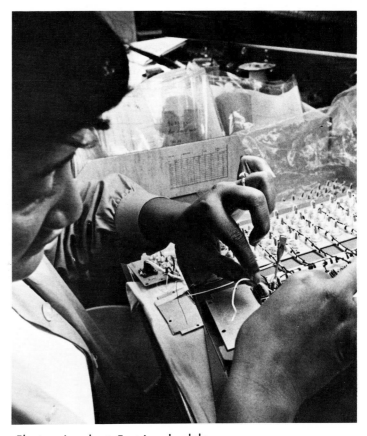

Electronics plant, Fort Lauderdale.

101

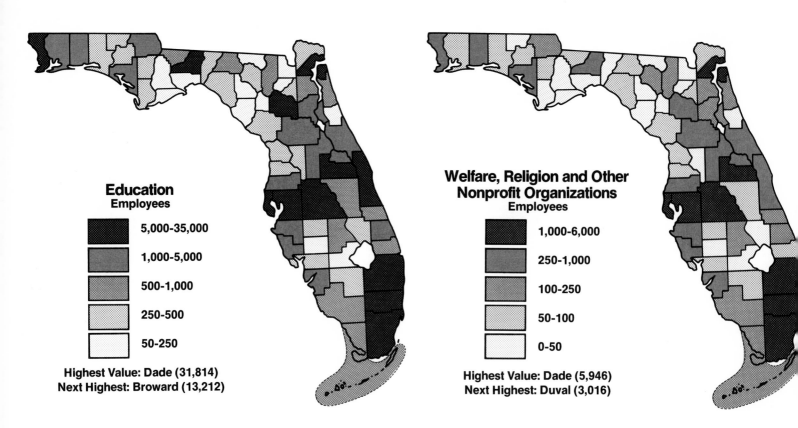

Education
Employees

5,000-35,000

1,000-5,000

500-1,000

250-500

50-250

Highest Value: Dade (31,814)
Next Highest: Broward (13,212)

**Welfare, Religion and Other
Nonprofit Organizations**
Employees

1,000-6,000

250-1,000

100-250

50-100

0-50

Highest Value: Dade (5,946)
Next Highest: Duval (3,016)

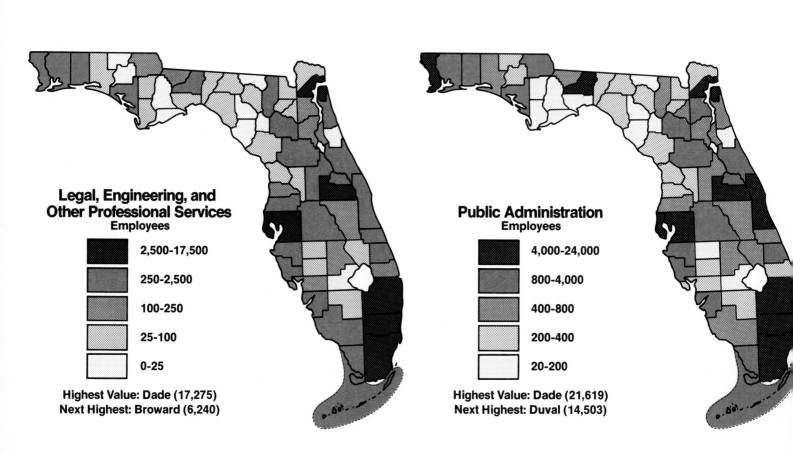

**Legal, Engineering, and
Other Professional Services**
Employees

2,500-17,500

250-2,500

100-250

25-100

0-25

Highest Value: Dade (17,275)
Next Highest: Broward (6,240)

Public Administration
Employees

4,000-24,000

800-4,000

400-800

200-400

20-200

Highest Value: Dade (21,619)
Next Highest: Duval (14,503)

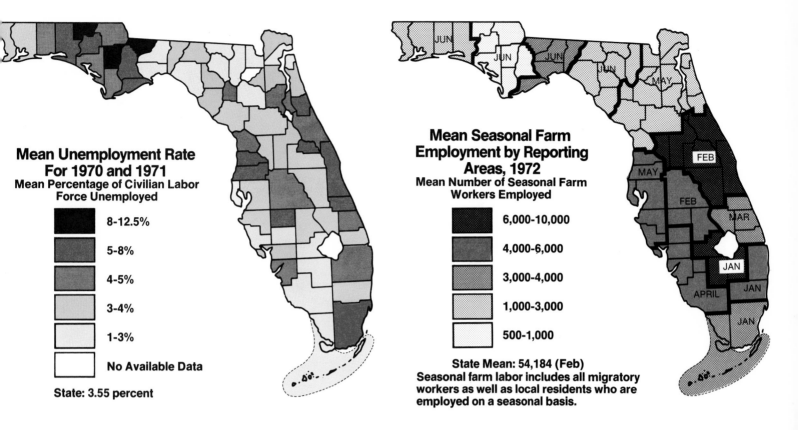

Mean Unemployment Rate For 1970 and 1971
Mean Percentage of Civilian Labor Force Unemployed

- 8-12.5%
- 5-8%
- 4-5%
- 3-4%
- 1-3%
- No Available Data

State: 3.55 percent

Mean Seasonal Farm Employment by Reporting Areas, 1972
Mean Number of Seasonal Farm Workers Employed

- 6,000-10,000
- 4,000-6,000
- 3,000-4,000
- 1,000-3,000
- 500-1,000

State Mean: 54,184 (Feb)
Seasonal farm labor includes all migratory workers as well as local residents who are employed on a seasonal basis.

This map should be interpreted with caution as significant fluctuation in unemployment rates is common from year to year. Therefore, because of the short time period represented (two years), the reader should not necessarily equate areas of high unemployment rates with chronic employment problems.

Unemployment Rates, 1952-1971

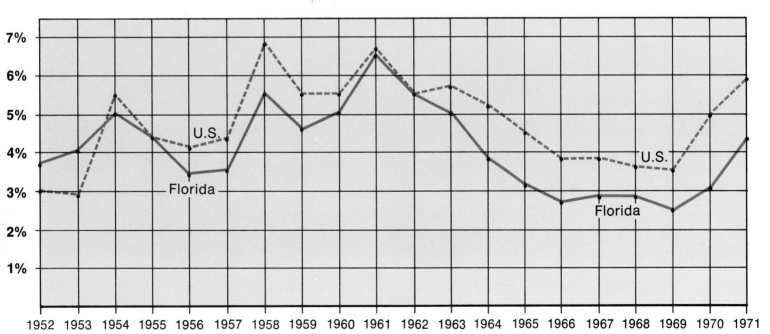

Health

Causes of Death — 1971

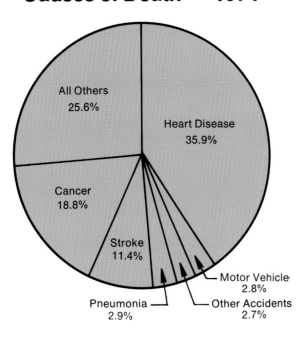

All Others
25.6%

Heart Disease
35.9%

Cancer
18.8%

Stroke
11.4%

Pneumonia
2.9%

Other Accidents
2.7%

Motor Vehicle
2.8%

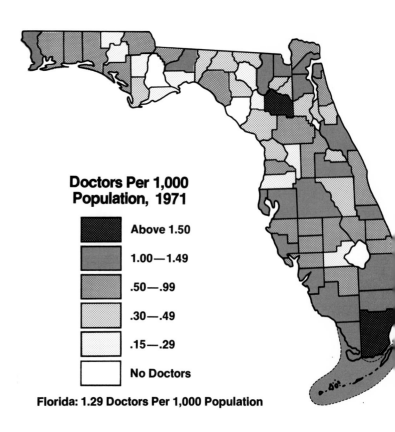

**Doctors Per 1,000
Population, 1971**

■	Above 1.50
	1.00 — 1.49
	.50 — .99
	.30 — .49
	.15 — .29
□	No Doctors

Florida: 1.29 Doctors Per 1,000 Population

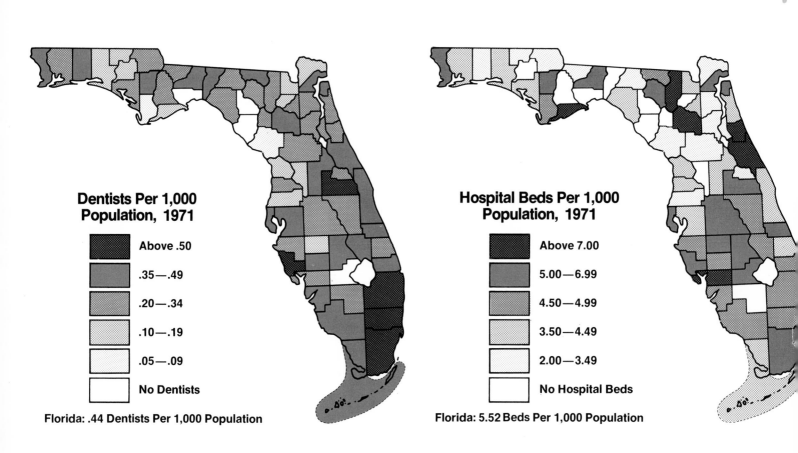

**Dentists Per 1,000
Population, 1971**

■	Above .50
	.35 — .49
	.20 — .34
	.10 — .19
	.05 — .09
□	No Dentists

Florida: .44 Dentists Per 1,000 Population

**Hospital Beds Per 1,000
Population, 1971**

■	Above 7.00
	5.00 — 6.99
	4.50 — 4.99
	3.50 — 4.49
	2.00 — 3.49
□	No Hospital Beds

Florida: 5.52 Beds Per 1,000 Population

History

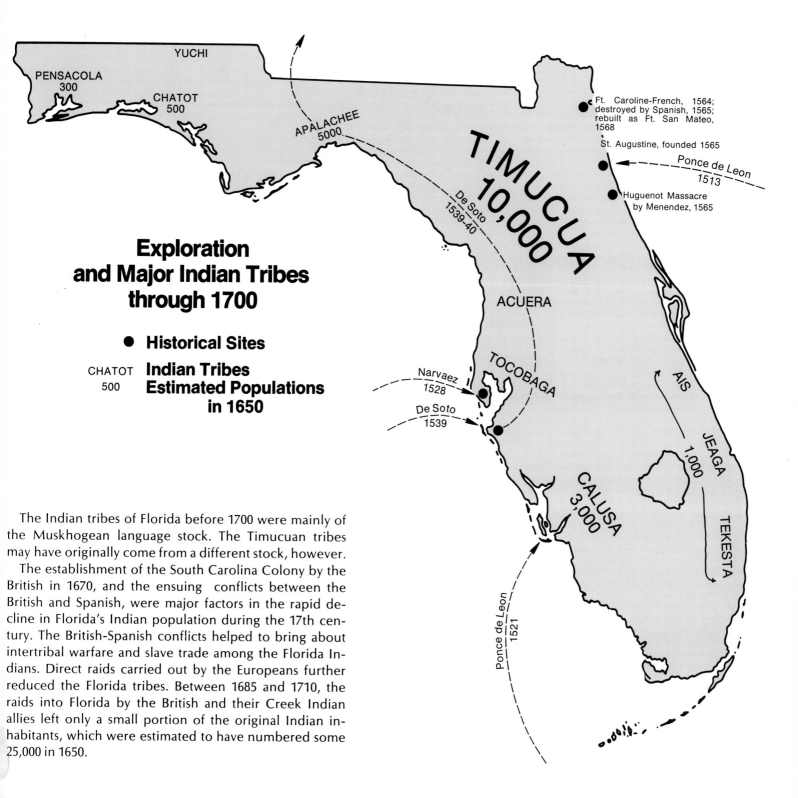

Exploration and Major Indian Tribes through 1700

● **Historical Sites**

CHATOT **Indian Tribes**
500 **Estimated Populations in 1650**

YUCHI

PENSACOLA
300

CHATOT
500

APALACHEE
5000

TIMUCUA
10,000

De Soto
1539-40

Ft. Caroline-French, 1564; destroyed by Spanish, 1565; rebuilt as Ft. San Mateo, 1568

St. Augustine, founded 1565

Ponce de Leon
1513

Huguenot Massacre
by Menendez, 1565

ACUERA

Narvaez
1528

TOCOBAGA

De Soto
1539

AIS

JEAGA
1,000

TEKESTA

CALUSA
3,000

Ponce de Leon
1521

The Indian tribes of Florida before 1700 were mainly of the Muskhogean language stock. The Timucuan tribes may have originally come from a different stock, however.

The establishment of the South Carolina Colony by the British in 1670, and the ensuing conflicts between the British and Spanish, were major factors in the rapid decline in Florida's Indian population during the 17th century. The British-Spanish conflicts helped to bring about intertribal warfare and slave trade among the Florida Indians. Direct raids carried out by the Europeans further reduced the Florida tribes. Between 1685 and 1710, the raids into Florida by the British and their Creek Indian allies left only a small portion of the original Indian inhabitants, which were estimated to have numbered some 25,000 in 1650.

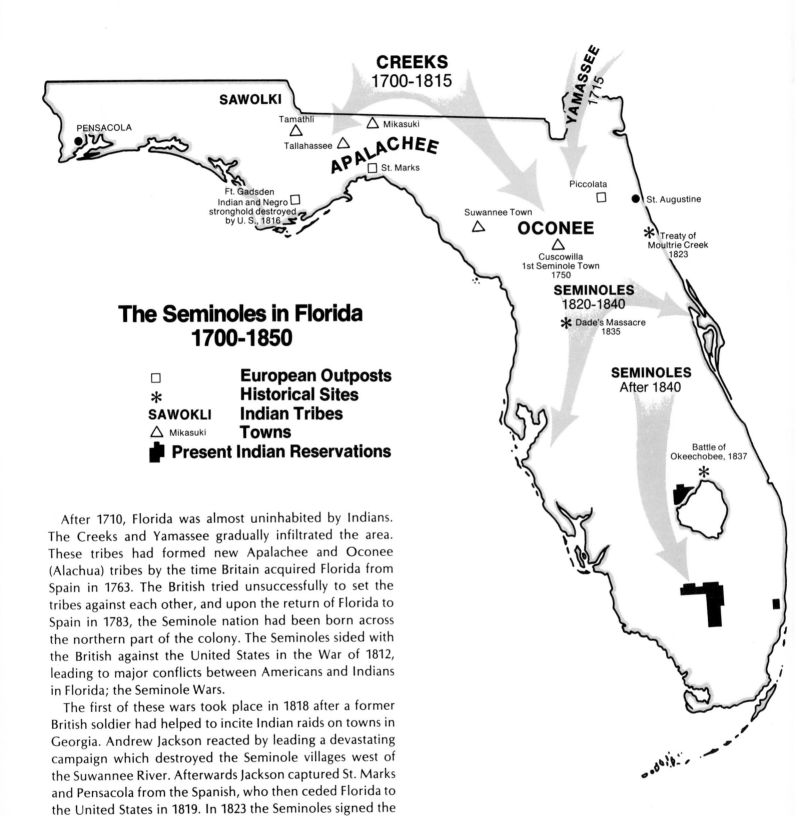

The Seminoles in Florida
1700-1850

□   **European Outposts**
*   **Historical Sites**
SAWOKLI   **Indian Tribes**
△ Mikasuki   **Towns**
▐   **Present Indian Reservations**

After 1710, Florida was almost uninhabited by Indians. The Creeks and Yamassee gradually infiltrated the area. These tribes had formed new Apalachee and Oconee (Alachua) tribes by the time Britain acquired Florida from Spain in 1763. The British tried unsuccessfully to set the tribes against each other, and upon the return of Florida to Spain in 1783, the Seminole nation had been born across the northern part of the colony. The Seminoles sided with the British against the United States in the War of 1812, leading to major conflicts between Americans and Indians in Florida; the Seminole Wars.

The first of these wars took place in 1818 after a former British soldier had helped to incite Indian raids on towns in Georgia. Andrew Jackson reacted by leading a devastating campaign which destroyed the Seminole villages west of the Suwannee River. Afterwards Jackson captured St. Marks and Pensacola from the Spanish, who then ceded Florida to the United States in 1819. In 1823 the Seminoles signed the Treaty of Moultrie Creek by which they ceded their lands in northern Florida and were relocated on reservations in central Florida.

The Seminoles, and Negroes with them, were greatly dissatisfied. In 1832, James Gadsden was appointed Indian commissioner and was ordered to force the Indians out of Florida and make more room for settlers. When President Jackson commanded the Indians to leave for reservations in Oklahoma, most of the chiefs refused, and new conflicts began. The Seminoles, led by the warrior Osceola, attacked United States forces in 1835. Osceola was captured and the Seminoles were largely defeated in 1837.

By 1840, four thousand Indians had been transported to Oklahoma and most of the several hundred remaining in the Everglades had been rounded up and sent west by 1854.

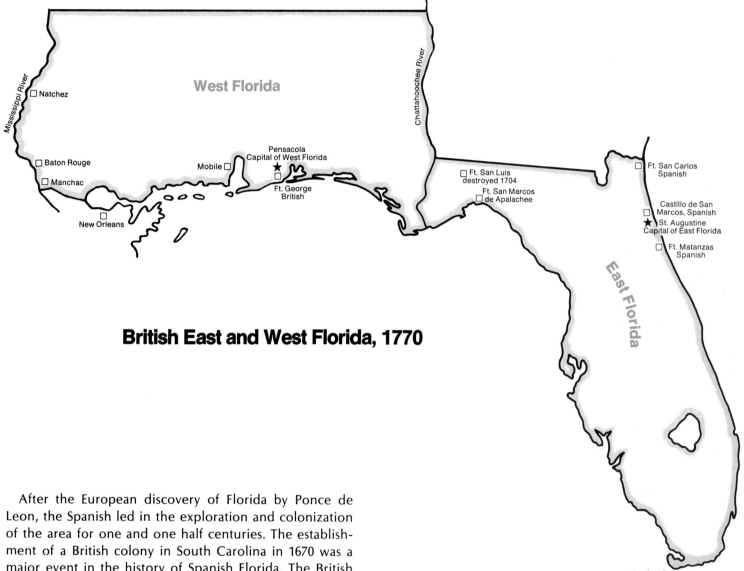

British East and West Florida, 1770

After the European discovery of Florida by Ponce de Leon, the Spanish led in the exploration and colonization of the area for one and one half centuries. The establishment of a British colony in South Carolina in 1670 was a major event in the history of Spanish Florida. The British penetrated into Spanish territory, set Indian tribes against each other, attacked the Spaniards persistently, and finally acquired Florida from Spain in exchange for Havana, Cuba.

The English developed new plantations of rice, indigo, and citrus across East and West Florida. West Florida extended to the Mississippi River and northward to latitude 32°28', as defined by a Royal Charter of 1764. Both Floridas remained loyal to England during the American Revolution, but they were returned by the British to Spain in 1783.

Following the return of Florida to Spain in 1783, the Spanish were plagued both by the Seminole Indians and by their new neighbor to the north, the United States. Spain yielded to the United States its claim to the part of West Florida north of latitude 31°11' by a treaty in 1795, though the Mississippi River continued to be the western boundary of Spanish Florida.

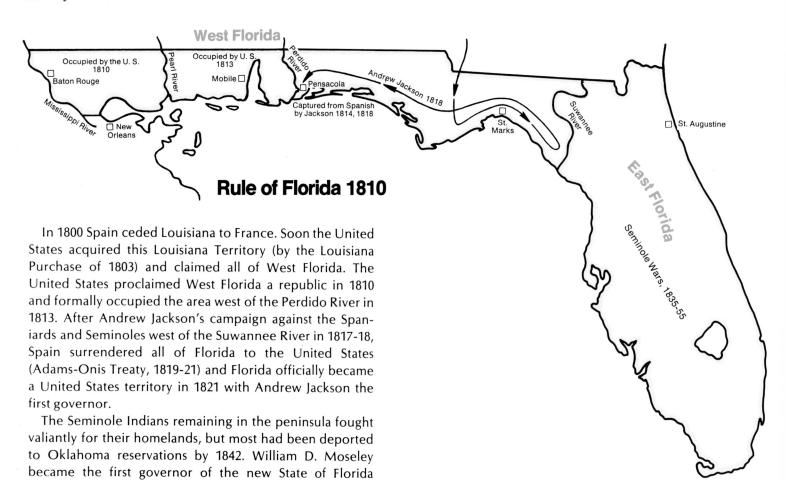

Rule of Florida 1810

In 1800 Spain ceded Louisiana to France. Soon the United States acquired this Louisiana Territory (by the Louisiana Purchase of 1803) and claimed all of West Florida. The United States proclaimed West Florida a republic in 1810 and formally occupied the area west of the Perdido River in 1813. After Andrew Jackson's campaign against the Spaniards and Seminoles west of the Suwannee River in 1817-18, Spain surrendered all of Florida to the United States (Adams-Onis Treaty, 1819-21) and Florida officially became a United States territory in 1821 with Andrew Jackson the first governor.

The Seminole Indians remaining in the peninsula fought valiantly for their homelands, but most had been deported to Oklahoma reservations by 1842. William D. Moseley became the first governor of the new State of Florida in 1845.

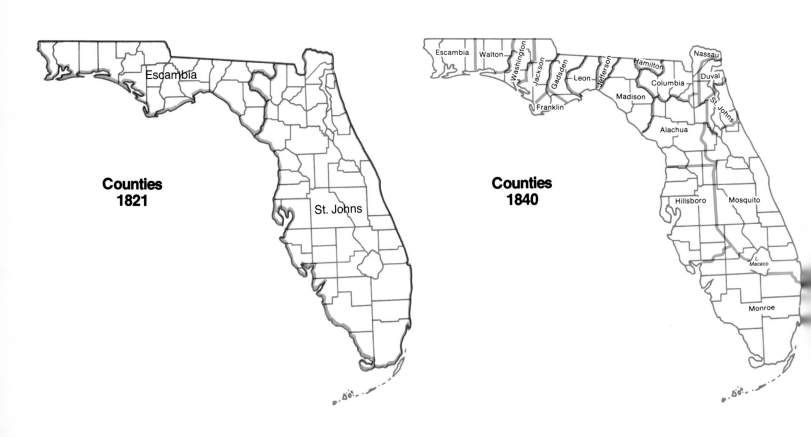

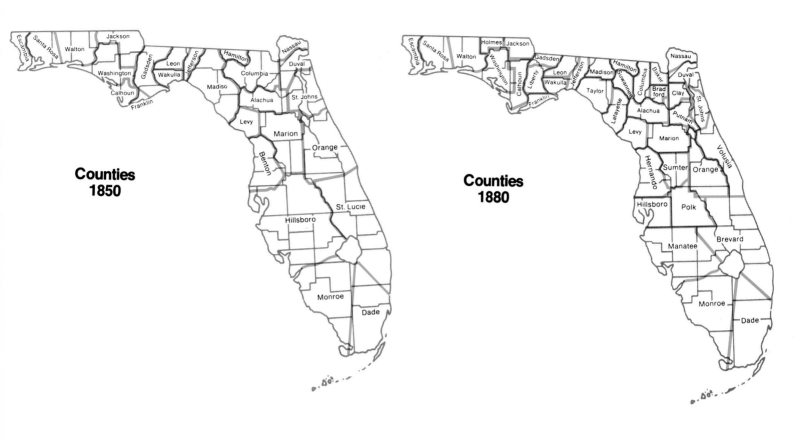

Counties 1850

Counties 1880

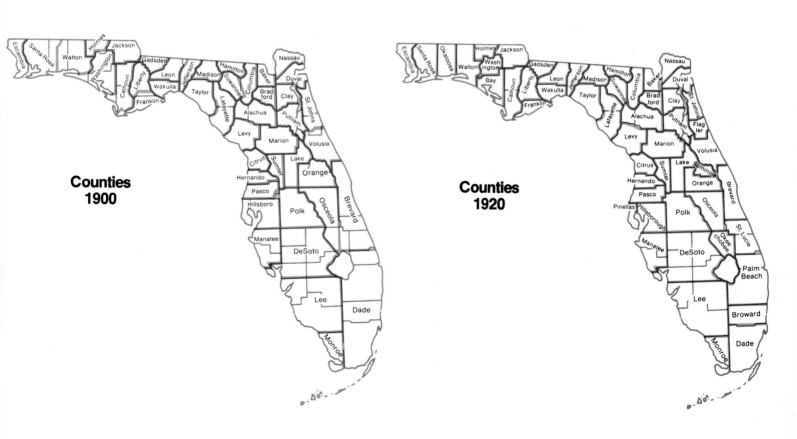

Counties 1900

Counties 1920

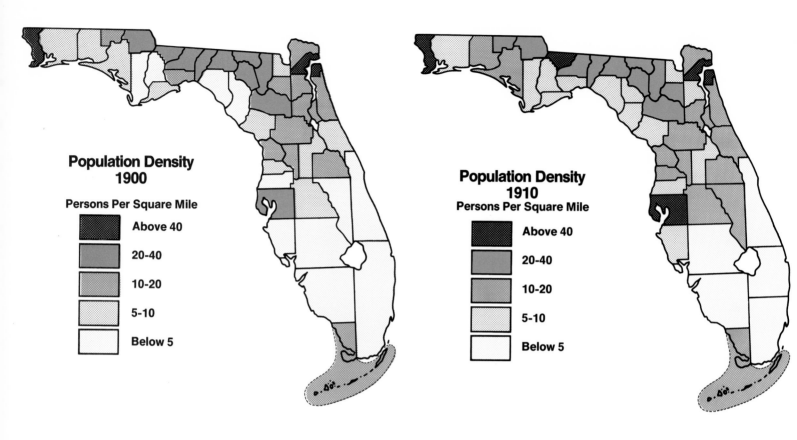

Population Density 1900

Persons Per Square Mile

- Above 40
- 20-40
- 10-20
- 5-10
- Below 5

Population Density 1910

Persons Per Square Mile

- Above 40
- 20-40
- 10-20
- 5-10
- Below 5

A rural home in north Florida, 1885

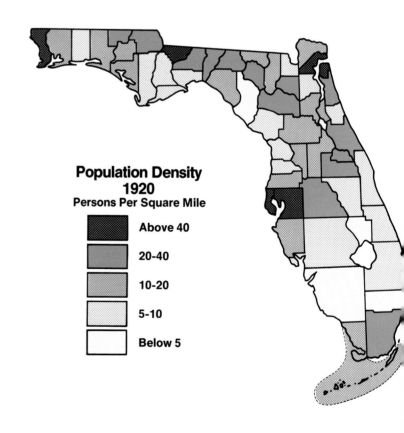

Population Density 1920

Persons Per Square Mile

- Above 40
- 20-40
- 10-20
- 5-10
- Below 5

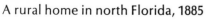

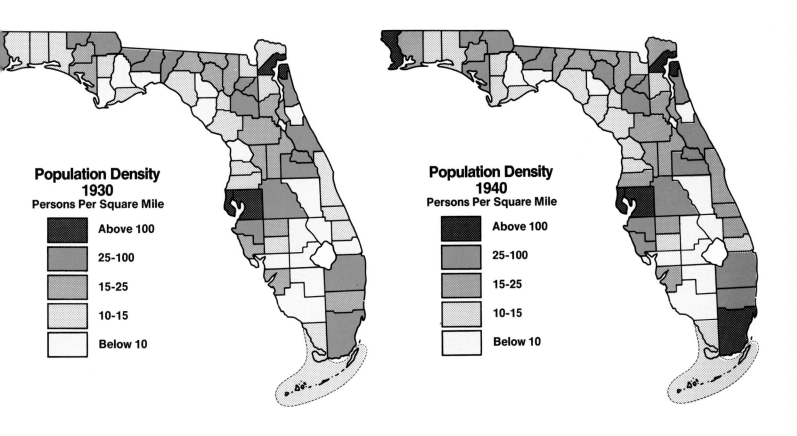

**Population Density
1930**
Persons Per Square Mile

- Above 100
- 25-100
- 15-25
- 10-15
- Below 10

**Population Density
1940**
Persons Per Square Mile

- Above 100
- 25-100
- 15-25
- 10-15
- Below 10

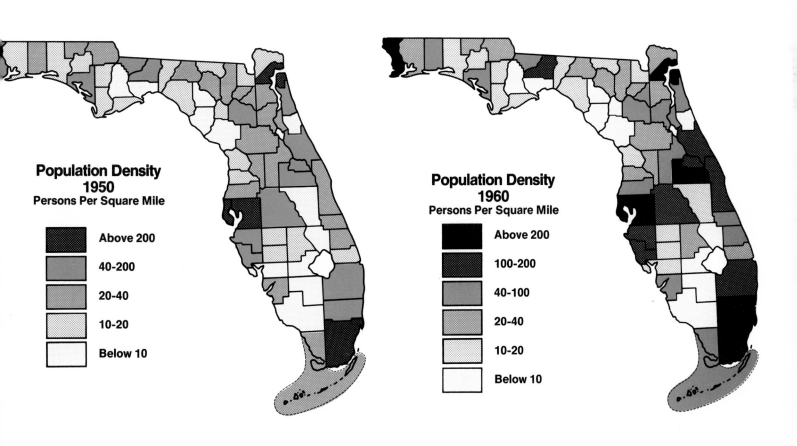

**Population Density
1950**
Persons Per Square Mile

- Above 200
- 40-200
- 20-40
- 10-20
- Below 10

**Population Density
1960**
Persons Per Square Mile

- Above 200
- 100-200
- 40-100
- 20-40
- 10-20
- Below 10

Population density for 1970 is shown on page 11.

Topographic Mapping

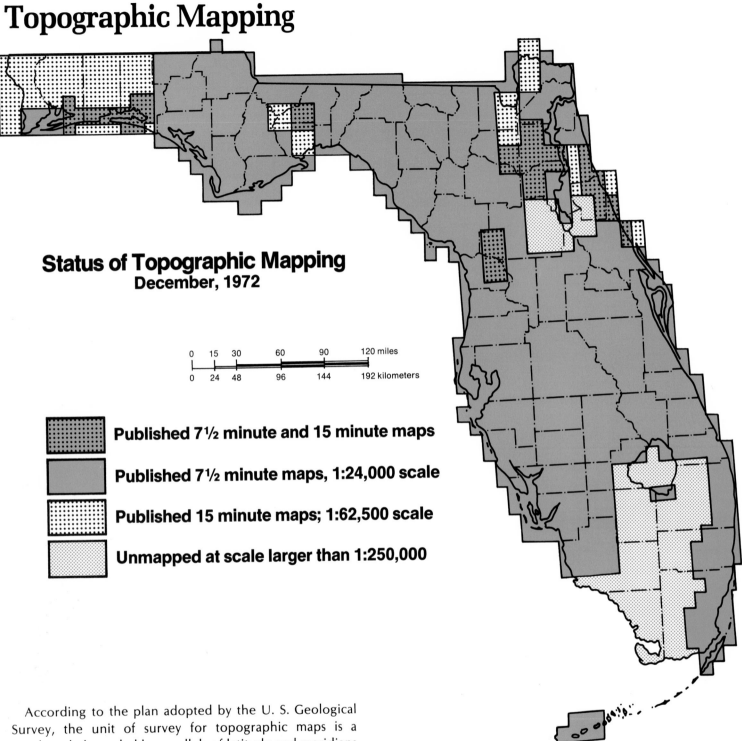

Status of Topographic Mapping
December, 1972

| 0 | 15 | 30 | 60 | 90 | 120 miles |
| 0 | 24 | 48 | 96 | 144 | 192 kilometers |

Published 7½ minute and 15 minute maps

Published 7½ minute maps, 1:24,000 scale

Published 15 minute maps; 1:62,500 scale

Unmapped at scale larger than 1:250,000

According to the plan adopted by the U. S. Geological Survey, the unit of survey for topographic maps is a quadrangle bounded by parallels of latitude and meridians of longitude. Quadrangles covering 7½ minutes of latitude and longitude are published at the scale of 1:24,000 (1 inch = 2,000 feet). Quadrangles covering 15 minutes of latitude and longitude are published at the scale of 1:62,500 (1 inch = approximately 1 mile). Each quadrangle is designated by the name of a city, town or prominent natural feature.

Topographic maps may be ordered from:

Distribution Section
U. S. Geological Survey
1200 South Eads Street
Arlington, Virginia 22202

The cost is 75 cents per copy, with the exception of 1:250,-000 scale maps which cost 1 dollar. Topographic quadrangle maps may also be purchased from local dealers, sporting goods stores, bookstores, etc. Dealer prices may be higher than Survey prices.

Aerial Photography

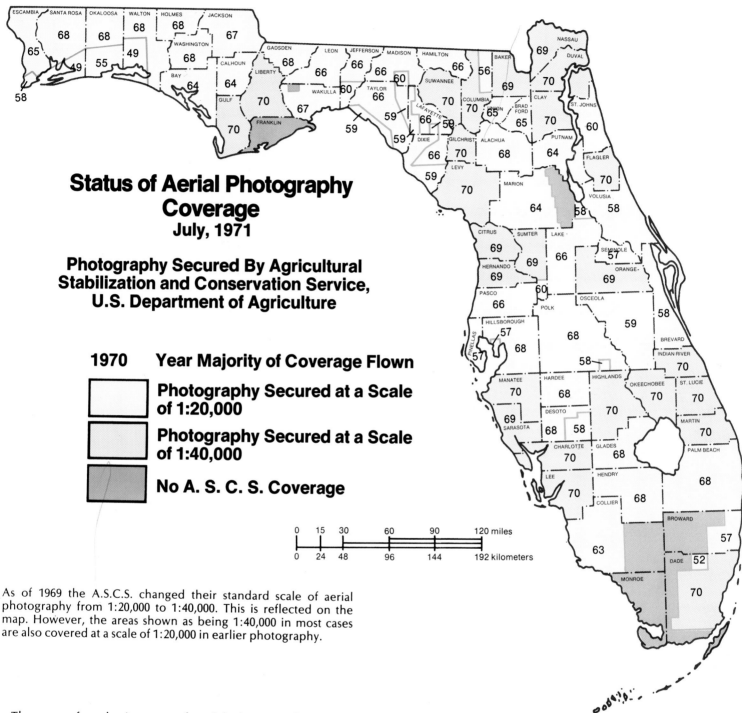

Status of Aerial Photography Coverage
July, 1971

Photography Secured By Agricultural Stabilization and Conservation Service, U.S. Department of Agriculture

1970   Year Majority of Coverage Flown

Photography Secured at a Scale of 1:20,000

Photography Secured at a Scale of 1:40,000

No A. S. C. S. Coverage

| 0 | 15 | 30 | 60 | 90 | 120 miles |
| 0 | 24 | 48 | 96 | 144 | 192 kilometers |

As of 1969 the A.S.C.S. changed their standard scale of aerial photography from 1:20,000 to 1:40,000. This is reflected on the map. However, the areas shown as being 1:40,000 in most cases are also covered at a scale of 1:20,000 in earlier photography.

There are four basic types of aerial photography: panchromatic (normal black and white), standard color, black and white infrared, and color infrared. Panchromatic coverage, at present, is the most extensive and cheapest to obtain.

Aerial photography by the A.S.C.S. represents the most comprehensive vertical coverage of Florida by a federal agency. The Soil Conservation Service, U.S. Forest Service, U.S. Coast Guard and U.S. Geological Survey also have partial coverage. In addition, the National Aeronautics and Space Administration (NASA) has obtained satellite and high altitude imagery covering selected areas of Florida.

There is no central laboratory from which reproductions of all government aerial photography can be purchased. Inquiries should be directed to the respective agency.

Requests for information regarding A.S.C.S. aerial photography in Florida should be addressed to:

Eastern Aerial Photography Laboratory
A.S.C.S. - U.S.D.A.
45 South French Broad Avenue
Asheville, North Carolina 28801

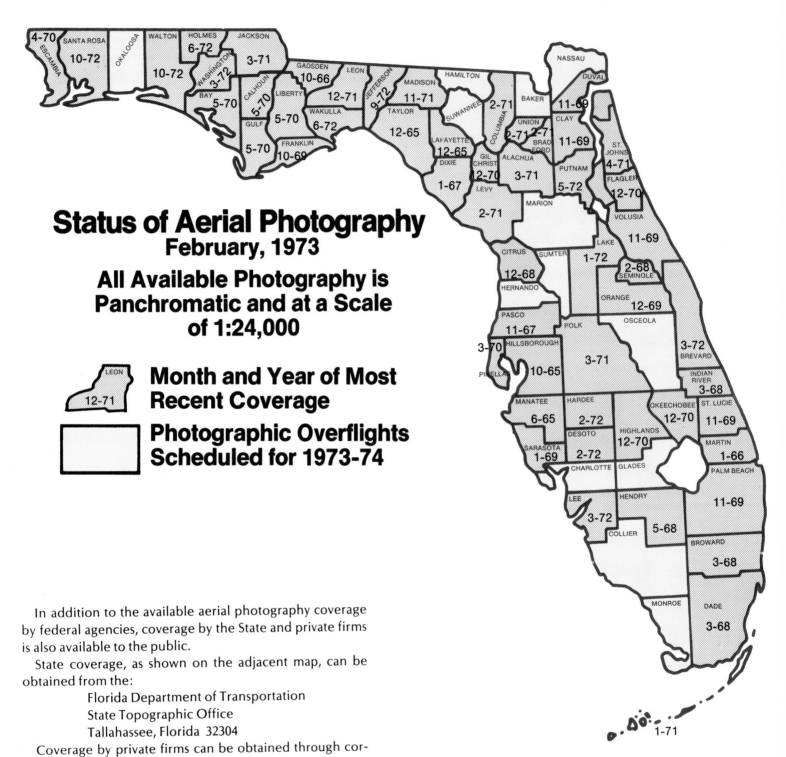

Status of Aerial Photography
February, 1973

All Available Photography is Panchromatic and at a Scale of 1:24,000

Month and Year of Most Recent Coverage

Photographic Overflights Scheduled for 1973-74

In addition to the available aerial photography coverage by federal agencies, coverage by the State and private firms is also available to the public.

State coverage, as shown on the adjacent map, can be obtained from the:

Florida Department of Transportation
State Topographic Office
Tallahassee, Florida 32304

Coverage by private firms can be obtained through correspondence with the individual firm.

An example of airborne imagery available through a commercial firm is a recent project executed by MARK HURD AERIAL SURVEYS, INC. In the period of October 1972 to February 1973, they obtained complete coverage of Florida in color infrared at a scale of 1:80,000. A six inch Zeiss metric camera was used and the mission was flown at an altitude of 40,000 feet. In addition to having the complete coverage in color infrared, the photos are available in rectified, 1:24,000, black and white reproducibles on a transparent base which are centered on standard 7½ minute topographic quadrangles. The utility of this project is obvious. Outdated topographic maps can be quickly brought up to date without extensive field work. Additionally, the detailed information can be easily measured with the respective quadrangles resulting in a tremendous asset to modern efforts in regional planning.

List of Sources

All maps, charts, and graphs are listed in bold face type in page number order. Page numbers are also in bold face. Sources are listed after the map, chart, or graph name. A source that used for more than one map, graph, or chart on a page is cited only once under the names of the graphs, charts, or maps.

Population

10. Census Year of Greatest Population. "Year of Maximum Population by Counties of the United States," Bureau of the Census, U.S. Department of Commerce, U.S. Maps, GE-50, No. 37.

Percentage of Population Change, 1960-70. *Florida Statistical Abstract, 1971*, Bureau of Economic and Business Research, College of Business Administration, University of Florida, University of Florida Press, Table 2.112.

Population Projection, 1978. *Florida Statistical Abstract, 1971*, Bureau of Economic and Business Research, College of Business Administration, University of Florida, University of Florida Press, Table 2.172.

11. Population Density by County, 1970. "Population Density by Counties of the United States, 1970," Bureau of the Census, U.S. Department of Commerce, U.S. Maps, GE-50, No. 38.

12. Standard Metropolitan Statistical Areas. *Florida Statistical Abstract, 1971*, Bureau of Economic and Business Research, College of Business Administration, University of Florida, University of Florida Press, Table 2.112.

13. Population Increase: Standard Metropolitan Statistical Areas (3 graphs). 14th-19th Decennial Censuses of the United States, "Census of Population, General Population Characteristics, Florida," Bureau of the Census, U.S. Department of Commerce.

14. Population Distribution. Preliminary map of "Population Distribution, Urban and Rural, in the United States: 1970," Bureau of the Census, U.S. Department of Commerce.

15. Rate of Natural Change, 1970. "Annual Report," Division of Health, Florida Department of Health and Rehabilitative Services, 1971.

Birth Rates for Whites, 1970.
Birth Rates for Non-Whites, 1970. "Annual Report," Division of Health, Florida Department of Health and Rehabilitative Services, 1971, Table 10.

16. Death Rates for Non-Whites, 1970.
Death Rates for Whites, 1970. "Annual Report," Division of Health, Florida Department of Health and Rehabilitative Services, 1971, Table 10.

Infant Mortality for Non-Whites, 1967-70, Average.
Infant Mortality for Whites, 1967-70, Average. "Annual Report," Division of Health, Florida Department of Health and Rehabilitative Services, editions 1968-71.

17. Florida's Birth and Death Rates, 1917-69. "Florida Vital Statistics, 1969," Division of Health, Florida Department of Health and Rehabilitative Services, figures 2 and 4.

Florida's and the Nation's Rates of Natural Change, 1917-1970. "Florida Vital Statistics," Division of Health, Florida Department of Health and Rehabilitative Services, 1969 and 1970.

18. Birthplace of Florida Residents. "1970 Census of Population, General Social and Economic Characteristics, Florida," Bureau of the Census, U.S. Department of Commerce, Table 50.

Percentage Urban, 1970. *Florida Statistical Abstract, 1971*, Bureau of Economic and Business Research, College of Business Administration, University of Florida, University of Florida Press, Table 2.122.

Florida Percentage Urban, 1880-1970. 10th-19th Decennial Censuses of the United States, "Census of Population, General Population Characteristics, Florida," Bureau of the Census, U.S. Department of Commerce.

Percentage Non-White, 1970. *Florida Statistical Abstract, 1971*, Bureau of Economic and Business Research, College of Business Administration, University of Florida, University of Florida Press, Table 2.142.

Florida Percentage Non-White, 1860-1970. 8th-19th Decennial Censuses of the United States, "Census of Population, General Population Characteristics, Florida," Bureau of the Census, U.S. Department of Commerce.

19. Percentage of Population under 18, 1970.
Percentage of Population 18-64, 1970.
Percentage of Population 65 and Over, 1970. Florida Statistical Abstract, 1971, Bureau of Economic and Business Administration, University of Florida, Table 2.252.

Population Pyramid, Florida, 1970. "1970 Census of Population, General Population Characteristics, Florida," Bureau of the Census, U.S. Department of Commerce.

Housing

20. Median Value of All Owner-Occupied Housing Units, 1970.
Median Value of Non-White Owner-Occupied Housing Units, 1970. "1970 Census of Housing, Detailed Housing Characteristics, Florida," Bureau of the Census, U.S. Department of Commerce.

21. Percentage of White Housing Units that are Owner-Occupied, 1970.
Percentage of Non-White Housing Units that are Owner-Occupied, 1970.
Percentage of White Housing Units that are Renter-Occupied, 1970.
Percentage of Non-White Housing Units that are Renter-Occupied, 1970. Florida Statistical Abstract, 1971, Bureau of Economic and Business Research, College of Business Administration, University of Florida, University of Florida Press, Table 8.092.

22. Percentage of Housing Units Seasonally Occupied, 1970. "1970 Census of Housing, Detailed Housing Characteristics, Florida," Bureau of the Census, U.S. Department of Commerce, Table 60.

Mobile Homes as a Percentage of all Housing Units, 1970. "1970 Census of Housing, Detailed Housing Characteristics, Florida," Bureau of the Census, U.S. Department of Commerce, Table 62.

23. Percentage Change in Apartments and Rooming House Rental Units, 1960-70. Hotel and Restaurant Division, Florida, Department of Business Regulation.

Median Monthly Rent of Occupied Housing Units, 1970. "1970 Census of Housing, Detailed Housing Characteristics, Florida," Bureau of the Census, U.S. Department of Commerce, Table 61.

Persons Per Housing Unit, 1970. "1970 Census of Housing, Detailed Housing Characteristics, Florida," Bureau of the Census, U.S. Department of Commerce, Table 60.

Income

24. Per Capita Income, 1969.
Mean Family Income, 1969. "1970 Census of Population, General Social and Economic Characteristics, Florida," Bureau of the Census, U.S. Department of Commerce, Table 124.

25. Percentage of Families with Income Below Official Federal Poverty Line, 1969. "1970 Census of Population, General Social and Economic Characteristics, Florida." Bureau of the Census, U.S. Department of Commerce, Table 124.

Percentage of Income from Services, 1970.
Percentage of Income from Wholesale and Retail Trade, 1970. Office of Business Economics, Regional Economics Division, U.S. Department of Commerce, unpublished data.

26. Percentage of Income from Mining, 1970.
Percentage of Income from Manufacturing, 1970. Office of Business Economics, Regional Economics Division, U.S. Department of Commerce, unpublished data.

27. Percentage of Income from Contract Construction, 1970.
Percentage of Income from Transportation, Communications and Public Utilities, 1970.
Percentage of Income from Finance, Insurance and Real Estate, 1970.
Total Private Nonfarm Earnings, 1970. Office of Business Economics, Regional Economics Division, U.S. Department of Commerce, unpublished data.

28. Public Education Dollar by Legislative Appropriations, 1972-73.
Division of Public University Appropriations, 1972-73. Florida Department of Education.

29. Public and Private Institutions of Higher Learning, 1970. *Florida Statistical Abstract, 1971*, Bureau of Economic and Business Research, College of Business Administration, University of Florida, University of Florida Press, Table 4.211.

30. Average Daily Attendance, K-12, 1970-71.
Assessed Value of Non-Exempt Property Supporting each Pupil, K-12, 1971.
Expense Per Pupil, K-12, 1970-71.
Percentage Increase in Expense Per Pupil, K-12, 1961-71. Florida Department of Education.

31. Sources of Revenue for Education. *Florida Statistical Abstract, 1971*, Bureau of Economic and Business Research, College of Business Administration, University of Florida, University of Florida Press, Tables 4.472 and 4.80.

Percentage of Public School Revenue from Local Sources, 1970-71.
Per Pupil Federal Revenue for Public Schools, 1970-71. Florida Department of Education.

32. Teacher's Salaries. *Statistical Abstract of the United States*, Bureau of the Census, U.S. Department of Commerce, 1950-1970.

Percentage of Pupils in Excess of Instruction Room Capacity, 1970-71. *Florida Statistical Abstract, 1971*, Bureau of Economic and Business Research, College of Business Administration, University of Florida, University of Florida Press, Table 4.162.

Change in Instructional Staff Salary, 1960-61 to 1970-71.
Average Annual Salary of Instructional Staff, 1970-71. Florida

Department of Education.

33. Percentage of Population 25 Years Old and Over with Less than Nine Years of Education, 1970.
Median School Years Completed for Persons 25 Years Old and Over, 1970. (Two maps: Male and Female) "1970 Census of Population, General Social and Economic Characteristics," Bureau of the Census, U.S. Department of Commerce, Table 120.

Government and Politics

34. Percentage of Voters Registered Democrat, 1972.
Percentage of Voters Registered Republican, 1972. "Registered Voters, State of Florida," Division of Elections, Florida Department of State, 1972.

35. Registered Voters, 1972. "Registered Voters, State of Florida," Division of Elections, Florida Department of State, 1972.

1972 Presidential Election. "Tabulations of the Official Votes in Florida, General Elections, 1972," Division of Elections, Florida Department of State, 1972.

1968 Presidential Election. "Tabulations of the Official Votes in Florida, General Elections, 1968," Division of Elections, Florida Department of State, 1968.

1964 Presidential Election. "Tabulations of the Official Votes in Florida, General Elections, 1964," Division of Elections, Florida Department of State, 1964.

36. 1960 Presidential Election. "Tabulations of the Official Votes in Florida, General Elections, 1960," Division of Elections, Florida Department of State, 1960.

1956 Presidential Election. "Tabulations of the Official Votes in Florida, General Elections, 1956," Division of Elections, Florida Department of State, 1956.

1952 Presidential Election. "Tabulations of the Official Votes in Florida, General Elections, 1952," Division of Elections, Florida Department of State, 1952.

1948 Presidential Election. "Tabulations of the Official Votes in Florida, General Elections, 1948." Division of Elections, Florida Department of State, 1948.

37. Federal Congressional Districts, 1972.
Florida Senate Legislative Districts, 1972.
Florida House Legislative Districts, 1972. Office of the Secretary of State, State of Florida.

38. Judicial Circuits, 1972.
Federal Court Districts, 1972.
State Appellate Districts, 1972. Office of the Secretary of State, State of Florida.

39. Total Value of all Property in Counties, 1971.
County Millage Rates, 1971.
Sources of State Receipts, 1971.
Per Capita Government Revenue, 1970-71. Office of the Comptroller, State of Florida.

40. Expenditures of the Florida Tax Dollar from the General Revenue Fund, 1971-72. Office of the Comptroller, State of Florida.

Per Capita Expenditures by City and County Governments, 1971. "Revenue and Expenditure Data for City and County Governments in Florida," Department of Administration and Florida League of Cities, 1972, Appendix D.

Florida Budget Expenditures, 1961-1973. "Estimated Expenditures," Office of the Governor, State of Florida.

Physical Characteristics

41. Landforms. Puri, H. S., and R. O. Vernon, "Physiographic Map of Florida," Enclosure to "Special Publication No. 5 (Summary of the Geology of Florida and a Guidebook to the Classic Exposures)," State Board of Conservation, Division of Geology, Florida Geological Survey, 1964.

42. Geology. "Geologic Map of Florida," Division of Geology, Florida Board of Conservation, Florida Geological Survey, 1965.

43. Soils. Bryan, O. C., "Generalized Soil Map of Florida," Supplement to "The Soils of Florida," Florida Department of Agriculture, Bulletin No. 42, 1962.

44. Natural Vegetation. Davis, John H., "General Map of Natural Vegetation of Florida," Agricultural Experiment Station, Institute of Food and Agricultural Sciences, University of Florida, 1967.

45. Mineral Resources and Industries of Florida. Calver, James L., "Mineral Resources and Industries of Florida," Florida Geological Survey, 1956 (This map was updated through personal interview with specialists at the Florida Geological Survey).

46. Wave Energy and Average Breaker Heights. Tanner, W. F., Map drawn specifically for this Atlas, Department of Geology, Florida State University.

Water

47. Drainage Basins and Average Flow of Major Streams. "Average Flow of Major Streams," U.S. Geological Survey in cooperation with the Bureau of Geology, Florida Department of Natural Resources, Map Series No. 34, 1969, and Kenner, W. E., R. W. Pride and C. S. Conover, "Drainage Basins in Florida," U.S. Geological Survey in cooperation with the Division of Geology, Florida Board of Conservation, Map Series No. 28, 1967.

48. Seasonal Variation of Streamflow in Florida. "Seasonal Variation of Streamflow in Florida," U.S. Geological Survey in cooperation with the Bureau of Geology, Florida Department of Natural Resources, Map Series No. 31, 1969.

Annual Runoff in Florida. "Runoff in Florida," U.S. Geological Survey in cooperation with the Bureau of Geology, Florida Board of Conservation, Map Series No. 22, 1966.

49. Principal Aquifers and Potentiometric Surface. "Principal Aquifers in Florida," U.S. Geological Survey, Division of Geology, Florida Board of Conservation, Map Series No. 16, 1965, and "Potentiometric Surface, Floridan Aquifer," Insert Map to "Depth to Base of Potable Water in the Floridan Aquifer," U.S. Geological Survey in cooperation with the Bureau of Geology, Florida Department of Natural Resources, Map Series No. 42, 1971.

50. Depth to Base of Potable Water in the Floridan Aquifer. "Depth to Base of Potable Water in the Floridan Aquifer," U.S. Geological Survey in cooperation with the Bureau of Geology, Florida Department of Natural Resources, Map Series No. 42, 1971.

51. Major Florida Springs. "Springs of Florida," U.S. Geological Survey, Bulletin No. 31, 1947.

Hardness of Water from Upper Part of the Floridan Aquifer.
Non-Carbonate Hardness of Water from the Floridan Aquifer. "Hardness of Water from the Upper Part of the Floridan Aquifer in Florida," U.S. Geological Survey in cooperation with the Florida Geological Survey, Division of Geology, Florida Board of Conservation, Map Series No. 13, 1965.

52. Dissolved Solids in Water from the Upper Part of the Floridan Aquifer.
Predominant Constituents. "Dissolved Solids in Water from the Upper Part of the Floridan Aquifer in Florida," U.S. Geological Survey in cooperation with the Florida Geological Survey, Division of Geology, Florida Board of Conservation, Map Series No. 4, 1965.

53. Chloride Concentration in Water from the Upper Part of the Floridan Aquifer. "Chloride Concentration in Water from the Upper Part of the Floridan Aquifer in Florida," U.S. Geological Survey in cooperation with the Florida Geological Survey, Division of Geology, Florida Board of Conservation, Map Series No. 12, 1965.

Sulfate Concentration in Water from the Upper Part of the Floridan Aquifer. "Sulfate Concentration in Water from the Upper Part of the Floridan Aquifer in Florida," U.S. Geological Survey in cooperation with the Florida Geological Survey, Division of Geology, Florida Board of Conservation, Map Series No. 15, 1965.

54. Generalized Distribution and Concentration of Orthophosphate in Florida Streams. "Generalized Distribution and Concentration of Orthophosphate in Florida Streams," U.S. Geological Survey in cooperation with the Bureau of Geology, Florida Department of Natural Resources, Map Series No. 33, 1969.

55. Total Fresh Water Withdrawn, by County, 1970. U.S. Geological Survey in cooperation with the Bureau of Geology, Florida Department of Natural Resources, unpublished data.

Florida's Fresh Water Withdrawal, 1950-70.
United States' Fresh Water Withdrawal, 1950-70. "Estimated Use of Water in the United States in 1970," Geological Survey Circular 676, Geological Survey, U.S. Department of the Interior, editions 1950-70.

56. Fresh Water Withdrawal Use in Florida, 1970.
Use for Self Supplied Industrial.
Use for Public Supply.
Use for Irrigation.
Use for Thermoelectric Power Generation. Advanced water use data, U.S. Geological Survey in cooperation with the Bureau of Geology, Florida Department of Natural Resources, unpublished data.

Climate

57. Mean Annual Temperature. "Climate of Florida," Climatography of the U.S., No. 60-8, (Climate of the States), U.S. Department of Commerce, National Oceanic and Atmospheric Administrative Environmental Data Service, Silver Spring, Maryland, 1972, pp 13-14 (text, pp. 1-2).

58. Extreme Highest and Lowest Recorded Temperatures. "Climate of Florida," Climatography of the U.S., No. 60-8, (Climate of the States), U.S. Department of Commerce, National Oceanic and Atmospheric Administrative Environmental Data Service, Silver Spring, Maryland, 1972, pp. 15-20, 22-55.

Mean January Temperature.

Mean July Temperature. "Climate of Florida," Climatography of the U.S., No. 60-8, (Climate of the States), U.S. Department of Commerce, National Oceanic and Atmospheric Administrative Environmental Data Service, Silver Spring, Maryland, 1972, pp. 13-14 (text, p. 2).

59. Mean Maximum Temperature, January.
Mean Minimum Temperature, January.
Mean Maximum Temperature, July.
Mean Minimum Temperature, July. "Climate of Florida," Climatography of the U.S., No. 60-8, (Climate of the States), U.S. Department of Commerce, National Oceanic and Atmospheric Administrative Environmental Data Service, Silver Spring, Maryland, 1972, pp. 13-14 (text, p. 2).

60. Normal Rainfall Variability by Month. "Climate of Florida," Climatography of the U.S., No. 60-8, (Climate of the States), U.S. Department of Commerce, National Oceanic and Atmospheric Administrative Environmental Data Service, Silver Spring, Maryland, 1972, pp. 15-20.

Mean Annual Rainfall. "Climate of Florida," Climatography of the U.S., No. 60-8, (Climate of the States), U.S. Department of Commerce, National Oceanic and Atmospheric Administrative Environmental Data Service, Silver Spring, Maryland, 1972, p. 21 (text, pp. 3-4).

61. Mean Winter Rainfall.
Mean Spring Rainfall. "Annual and Seasonal Rainfall in Florida," U.S. Geological Survey in cooperation with the Bureau of Geology, Florida Department of Natural Resources, Map Series No. 40, 1971 (text, "Climate of Florida," Climatography of the U.S., No. 60-8, (Climate of the States), U.S. Department of Commerce, National Oceanic and Atmospheric Administrative Environmental Data Service, Silver Spring, Maryland, 1972, pp. 3-4).

62. Mean Summer Rainfall.
Mean Autumn Rainfall. "Annual and Seasonal Rainfall in Florida," U.S. Geological Survey in cooperation with the Bureau of Geology, Florida Department of Natural Resources, Map Series No. 40, 1971 (text, "Climate of Florida," Climatography of the U.S., No. 60-8, (Climate of the States), U.S. Department of Commerce, National Oceanic and Atmospheric Administrative Environmental Data Service, Silver Spring, Maryland, 1972, pp. 3-4).

Mean Date of First Freeze Occurrence.
Mean Date of Last Freeze Occurrence. Sketch maps, State Climatologist, State of Florida.

63. Southeastern United States, Mean Annual Freeze-Free Period. "The National Atlas of the United States of America," Geological Survey, U.S. Department of the Interior, pp. 110-111.

64. Daytime Sunshine and Clouds.
Humidity and Fog.
Wind Direction and Velocity. Atlas of Florida, compiled by Erwin Raisz and Associates, text by John R. Dunkle, Department of Geography, University of Florida, University of Florida Press, 1964, pp. 12-13.

Tornado Frequency in Florida. "The Occurrence of Tornadoes in Florida," Climate Sheet No. 2, State Climatologist, State of Florida.

65. Frequency of Florida Hurricanes by Months from 1885-1965.
Points of Entry and Direction of Travel of All Hurricanes which have Affected Florida from 1885-1965.
Chance of a Hurricane Striking the Florida Coastline. "Florida Hurricanes," Weather Bureau Technical Memorandum SR-38, U.S. Department of Commerce, Environmental Science Services Administration, 1967.

Mean Frequency of Tornados by Months from 1959-71. "The Occurrence of Tornados in Florida," Climate Sheet No. 2, State Climatologist, State of Florida.

Transportation and Communication

66. 1971 Highway Traffic Flow. Division of Transportation Planning, Florida Department of Transportation, in cooperation with U.S. Department of Transportation, Federal Highway Administration, 1971.

67. Internal Airline Routes and Passenger Traffic, All Services, 1970. "Internal Airline Routes and Passenger Traffic, All Services, 1970," Federal Aviation Administration, U.S. Department of Transportation, Part I, Table B (for 12 months ended June 30, 1970). 2. Champion Map Corporation, Charlotte, North Carolina, 1972. "State of Florida Map."

68. Railroads, 1970. "State of Florida Map," Champion Map Corporation, Charlotte, North Carolina, 1972.

69. Florida Ports and Waterways. 1. "Waterborne Commerce of the U.S., 1970," Corps of Engineers, U.S. Department of the Army. 2. "Florida Ports and Waterways Directory, 1972," Division of Commercial Development, Florida Department of Commerce.

70. Major Newspapers, Daily Circulation, April 1972. Florida Statistical Abstract, 1972, Bureau of Economic and Business Research, College of Business Administration, University of Florida, University of Florida Press, Table 14.192.

71. Radio Stations, 1971. "TV and Radio Stations," Broadcasting 1972 Yearbook, Broadcasting Publications, Inc.

72. Television Stations, 1971. "TV and Radio Stations," Broadcasting 1972 Yearbook, Broadcasting Publications, Inc.

Tourism and Recreation

73. Origins of Incoming Tourists Traveling by Private Vehicle, 1971. "1971 Florida Tourist Study," Florida Department of Commerce, Table 4.

Destinations of Incoming Tourists Traveling by Private Vehicle, 1971. "1971 Florida Tourist Study," Florida Department of Commerce, Table 7.

74. Estimated Number of All Tourists Visiting Florida, 1933-70. "Florida Tourist Study," editions 1968-70, Florida Department of Commerce, Chart I.

Total Number of Tourists Entering Florida by Month, 1970. "1970 Florida Tourist Study," Florida Department of Commerce, Table 1.

Estimated Length of Stay, 1970. "1970 Florida Tourist Study," Florida Department of Commerce, Table 5.

75. Division of Tourist Dollar, 1968. "1969 Florida Tourist Study," Florida Department of Commerce, Chart 4.

Number of Hotel and Motel Rental Units, 1970.
Percentage Change in Hotel and Motel Rental Units, 1960-70. Hotel and Restaurant Division, Florida Department of Business Regulation.

76. State and National Parks, State Recreation Areas, National Monuments and Historical Memorials, and Canoe Trails, 1972. "State and Federal Outdoor Recreation Areas in Florida, 1971," Florida Department of Natural Resources, (updated by interview with Department personnel).

77. State and National Forests and Wildlife Preservation Areas, 1972. "State and Federal Outdoor Recreation Areas in Florida, 1971," Florida Department of Natural Resources (updated by interview with Department personnel).

78. Fishing Licenses Sold to Residents, 1970-71.
Fishing Licenses Sold to Non-Residents, 1970-71.
Hunting Licenses Sold to Residents, 1970-71.
Hunting Licenses Sold to Non-Residents, 1970-71. Game and Freshwater Fish Commission, Florida Department of Natural Resources.

Economic Activity

79. Land Use, 1970. Fernald, Edward A., Department of Geography, Florida State University.

Agriculture

80. Total Number of Farms, 1969.
Average Farm Size, 1969.
Part-Time Farms as a Percentage of All Farms, 1969.
Value of Farm Products Sold, 1969. "1969 Census of Agriculture," Bureau of the Census, U.S. Department of Commerce, Part 29, Florida, Section 2, County Data.

81. Number of Farms by Type, 1969.
Value of Farmland and Buildings per Acre, 1969.
Value of All Farm Products Sold, 1969. "1969 Census of Agriculture," Bureau of the Census, U.S. Department of Commerce, Part 29, Florida, Section 2, County Data.

Acreage Harvested, 1969-70. Florida Statistical Abstract, 1971, Bureau of Economic and Business Research, College of Business Administration, University of Florida, University of Florida Press, Table 10.331.

82. Percentage of Total Farm Area in Harvested Crops, 1969.
Percentage of Total Land in Farms, 1969. "1969 Census of Agriculture," Bureau of the Census, U.S. Department of Commerce, Part 29, Florida, Section 2, County Data.

Percentage of Total Land in Farms, 1950, 1959. "Census of Agriculture," Bureau of the Census, U.S. Department of Commerce.

83. Percentage of Total Land in Farms, 1900, 1920, 1930, 1940. "Census of Agriculture," Bureau of the Census, U.S. Department of Commerce.

84. Harvested Vegetable and Small Fruit Acreage, 1969. Florida Statistical Abstract, 1971, Bureau of Economic and Business Research, College of Business Administration, University of Florida, University of Florida Press, Table 10.331.

Vegetable, Potato, Berry and Melon Acreage, 1969.
Harvested Hay Acreage, 1969.
Commercial Fertilizer Pounds per Acre, 1969. "1969 Census of Agriculture," Bureau of the Census, U.S. Department of Commerce, Part 29, Florida, Section 2, County Data.

85. Percentage of Total Farmland Under Irrigation, 1969.
Value of Beef Cattle and Calves Sold, 1969.
Value of Dairy Products Sold, 1969.
Value of Poultry and Poultry Products, 1969. "1969 Census of Agriculture," Bureau of the Census, U.S. Department of Commerce, Part 29, Florida, Section 2, County Data.

86. Citrus Production 1945-46 to 1970-71. "Citrus Summary 1971," Florida Agricultural Statistics, Florida Department of Agriculture, Chart 1.

Total Estimated Citrus Production, 1970-71. "Citrus Summary 1971," Florida Agricultural Statistics, Florida Department of Agriculture, Table 40.

87. Value of Machinery per Cultivated Acre, 1969.
Number of Tractors per 1,000 Cultivated Acres, 1969.
Farm Production Expenditures, 1969. "1969 Census of Agriculture," Bureau of the Census, U.S. Department of Commerce, Part 29, Florida, Section 2, County Data.

88. Average per Farm Payments by Government Farm Programs, 1969.
Average Per Farm Value of all Agricultural Products Sold, 1969. "1969 Census of Agriculture," Bureau of the Census, U.S. Department of Commerce, Part 29, Florida, Section 2, County Data.

Forestry

88. Percentage of Total Land in Forest, 1970.
Predominant Timber Types, 1970. 1. "Forest Statistics for Northwest Florida, 1969," Southeastern Forest Experiment Station, Asheville, North Carolina, U.S.D.A. Forest Service, Resource Bulletin SE-14, Table 3. 2. "Forest Statistics for Northeast Florida, 1970," Southeastern Forest Experiment Station, Asheville, North Carolina, U.S.D.A. Forest Service, Resource Bulletin SE-15, Table 3. 3. "Forest Statistics for South Florida, 1970," Southeastern Forest Experiment Station, Asheville, North Carolina, U.S.D.A. Forest Service, Resource Bulletin SE-16, Table 3. 4. "Forest Statistics for Central Florida, 1970," Southeastern Forest Experiment Station, Asheville, North Carolina, U.S.D.A. Forest Service, Resource Bulletin SE-17, Table 3.

89. Percentage of Forest Acreage Needing Reforestation, 1970. "Work of the Service; Program, Problems, Progress," Florida Forest Service, Division of Forestry, Florida Department of Agriculture and Consumer Services.

Pine Seedlings Planted, 1951-71.
Acres Planted in Seedlings, 1928-71. Florida Forest Service, Division of Forestry, Florida Department of Agriculture and Consumer Services.

90. Pulpwood Production, 1970. Beltz, Roy C., "Southern Pulpwood Production, 1970," Southern Forest Experiment Station, New Orleans, Forest Service, U.S. Department of Agriculture, Resource Bulletin S0-28, 1971.

Ownership of Commercial Forest Areas, 1970.
Net Volume of Sawtimber Stand, 1970. 1. "Forest Statistics for Northwest Florida, 1969," Southeastern Forest Experiment Station, Asheville, North Carolina, U.S.D.A. Forest Service, Resource Bulletin SE-14, Table 3. 2. "Forest Statistics for Northeast Florida, 1970," Southeastern Forest Experiment Station, Asheville, North Carolina, U.S.D.A. Forest Service, Resource Bulletin SE-15, Table 3. 3. "Forest Statistics for South Florida, 1970," Southeastern Forest Experiment Station, Asheville, North Carolina, U.S.D.A. Forest Service, Resource Bulletin SE-16, Table 3. 4. "Forest Statistics for Central Florida, 1970," Southeastern Forest Experiment Station, Asheville, North Carolina, U.S.D.A. Forest Service, Resource Bulletin SE-17, Table 3.

Pulpwood and Lumber Production. "Forest Products Income Figures, Florida," Florida Forest Service, Division of Forestry, Florida Department of Agriculture and Consumer Services, 1968.

Commercial Fishing

91. Total Marine Landings. "Summary of Florida Commercial Marine Landings," Division of Marine Resources, Florida Department of Natural Resources, 1960-70 editions.

92. Value of Marine Landings.
Shrimp Catch, Average Annual Value, 1960-70. "Summary of Florida Commercial Marine Landings," Division of Marine Resources, Florida Department of Natural Resources, 1960-70 editions.

93. Fish Catch, Average Annual Value, 1960-70.
Shellfish Catch, Average Annual Value, 1960-70. "Summary of Florida Commercial Marine Landings," Division of Marine Resources, Florida Department of Natural Resources, 1960-70 editions.

Manufacturing

93. Value Added and Employment, 1947-69. *Florida Statistical Abstract,* Bureau of Economic and Business Research, College of Business Administration, University of Florida, University of Florida Press, editions 1967-71.

94. Value Added, 1967. "Area Statistics, 1967 Census of Manufactures," Bureau of the Census, U.S. Department of Commerce, Volume III, Part 1.

Percentage Change in Value Added, 1963-67. *Florida Statistical Abstract, 1971,* Bureau of Economic and Business Research, College of Business Administration, University of Florida, University of Florida Press, Table 12.122.

Number of Manufacturing Establishments, 1970.
Employment in Manufacturing, 1970. "1970 Census of Population, General Social and Economic Characteristics, Florida," Bureau of the Census, U.S. Department of Commerce, Table 123.

95. Employment in Furniture, Lumber, and Wood Products, 1970.
Percentage Change in Manufacturing Employment, 1960-70.
Employment in Metal Industries, 1970.

Employment in Machinery and Transportation Equipment, 1970. "1970 Census of Population, General Social and Economic Characteristics, Florida," Bureau of the Census, U.S. Department of Commerce, Table 123.

96. Employment in Other Durable Goods, 1970.
Employment in Food and Kindred Products, 1970.
Employment in Printing, Publishing and Allied Industries, 1970.
Employment in Textiles and Fabricated Textile Products, 1970. "1970 Census of Population, General Social and Economic Characteristics, Florida," Bureau of the Census, U.S. Department of Commerce, Table 123.

97. Employment in Chemicals and Allied Products, 1970.
Employment in Other Nondurable Goods, 1970. "1970 Census of Population, General Social and Economic Characteristics, Florida," Bureau of the Census, U.S. Department of Commerce, Table 123.

Employment

98. Employment, 1970.
Agriculture, Forestry and Fisheries.
Mining. "1970 Census of Population, General Social and Economic Characteristics, Florida," Bureau of the Census, U.S. Department of Commerce, Table 123.

99. Construction.
Employment in Manufacturing, 1970.
Machinery and Transportation Equipment.
Transportation and Communications. "1970 Census of Population, General Social and Economic Characteristics, Florida," Bureau of the Census, U.S. Department of Commerce, Table 123.

100. Wholesale Trade.
Retail Trade.
Banking, Insurance and Finance.
Business and Repair Services. "1970 Census of Population, General Social and Economic Characteristics, Florida," Bureau of the Census, U.S. Department of Commerce, Table 123.

101. Utilities and Sanitary Services.
Private Households and Other Personal Services.
Hospitals and Health Services. "1970 Census of Population, General Social and Economic Characteristics, Florida," Bureau of the Census, U.S. Department of Commerce, Table 123.

102. Education.
Welfare, Religion and Other Nonprofit Organizations.
Legal, Engineering, and Other Professional Services.
Public Administration. "1970 Census of Population, General Social and Economic Characteristics, Florida," Bureau of the Census, U.S. Department of Commerce, Table 123.

103. Unemployment Rates, 1952-71. "Manpower Report to the President," U.S. Department of Labor, 1972.

Mean Unemployment Rate for 1970 and 1971. *Florida Statistical Abstract, 1972,* Bureau of Economic and Business Research, College of Business Administration, University of Florida, University of Florida Press, Table 9.062.

Mean Seasonal Farm Employment by Reporting Areas, 1972. The Farm Labor and Rural Manpower Service, Division of Labor and Employment Opportunities, Florida, Department of Commerce.

Health

104. Causes of Death, 1971. "Annual Report, 1971," Division of Health, Florida Department of Health and Rehabilitative Services, Table 7.

Doctors Per 1,000 Population, 1971.
Dentists Per 1,000 Population, 1971.
Hospital Beds Per 1,000 Population, 1971. "Florida's Health Manpower," Bureau of Comprehensive Health Planning, Division of Planning and Evaluation, Department of Health and Rehabilitative Services, 1971, Table I.

History

105. Exploration and Major Indian Tribes Through 1700. 1. "Indians of Florida," Hearne Brothers Map Company. 2. Fairbanks, Charles H., "Ethnohistorical Report of the Florida Indians," Department of Anthropology, Florida State University.

106. The Seminoles in Florida, 1700-1850. 1. "Indians of Florida," Hearne Brothers Map Company. 2. Fairbanks, Charles H., "Ethnohistorical Report of the Florida Indians," Department of Anthropology, Florida State University. 3. Writings by J. R. Swanton, Marjory Stoneman Douglas, Charleton Tebeau, John K. Mahon, Charles Mowat. 4. Directive assistance and consultation by Hale G. Smith, Department of Anthropology, Florida State University and J. Leitch Wright, Department of History, Florida State University.

107. British East and West Florida, 1770. 1. "Indians of Florida," Hearne Brothers Map Company. 2. Fairbanks, Charles H., "Ethnohistorical Report of the Florida Indians," Department of Anthropology, Florida State University. 3. Writings by J. R. Swanton, Marjory Stoneman Douglas, Charleton Tebeau, John K. Mahon, Charles Mowat. 4. Directive assistance and consultation by Hale G. Smith, Department of Anthropology, Florida State University and J. Leitch Wright, Department of History, Florida State University.

108. Rule of Florida, 1810. 1. "Indians of Florida," Hearne Brothers Map Company. 2. Fairbanks, Charles H., "Ethnohistorical Report of the Florida Indians," Department of Anthropology, Florida State University. 3. Writings by J. R. Swanton, Marjory Stoneman Douglas, Charleton Tebeau, John K. Mahon, Charles Mowat. 4. Directive assistance and consultation by Hale G. Smith, Department of Anthropology, Florida State University and J. Leitch Wright, Department of History, Florida State University.

Counties, 1821, 1840. "Development of Counties in Florida," Historical Records and State Archives Surveys, Florida Works Progress Administration.

109. Counties, 1850, 1880, 1900, 1920. "Development of Counties in Florida," Historical Records and State Archives Surveys, Florida Works Progress Administration.

110. Population Density, 1900, 1910, 1920. 12th-15th Decennial Censuses of the United States, "Census of Population, General Population Characteristics, Florida," Bureau of the Census, U.S. Department of Commerce.

111. Population Density, 1930, 1940, 1950, 1960. 16th-18th Decennial Censuses of the United States, "Census of Population, General Population Characteristics, Florida," Bureau of the Census, U.S. Department of Commerce.

Topographic Mapping

112. Status of Topographic Mapping, December 1972. "Index to Topographic Maps of Florida," Geological Survey, U.S. Department of the Interior, 1972.

Aerial Photography

113. Status of Aerial Photography Coverage, 1971. Florida Index, "ASCS Aerial Photography Status Maps," Agricultural Stabilization and Conservation Service, U.S. Department of Agriculture, 1971.

114. Status of Aerial Photography Coverage, 1973. Photogrammetric Division, Florida Department of Transportation, 1972.

Back Cover

The picture of Florida on the back cover is a photo mosaic produced from images taken by the NASA Earth Resources Technology Satellite (ERTS-1) which has been in polar orbit around the earth since 23 July 1972. The mosaic is composed of 18 individual color composite prints, carefully matched and assembled to cover the entire state of Florida. ERTS color composites are produced from three separate black and white transparencies, each transparency representing a different spectral band. The original mosaic was prepared by the General Electric Photo Engineering Lab and photographic prints may be ordered by calling (301) 345-9344, or writing GE Photo Lab, 5030 Herzel Place, Beltsville, Maryland 20705.